Kingdoms of Man
and the
Kingdom of God

Richard S. Hanson

Augsburg Publishing House
Minneapolis, Minnesota

KINGDOMS OF MAN AND THE KINGDOM OF GOD

Quotations from *The Firmament of Time,* copyright 1960 by Loren Eiseley and copyright 1960 by the Trustees of the University of Pennsylvania, reprinted by permission of Atheneum Publishers.

Quotations from "The Book of Job," translated and edited by Marvin H. Pope, copyright 1965 by Doubleday & Company, Inc. and from "The Book of Jeremiah," translated and edited by John Bright, copyright 1965 by Doubleday & Company, Inc. reprinted from *The Anchor Bible* by permission of Doubleday & Company, Inc.

Quotations from *Psalms in Modern Speech* by Richard S. Hanson reprinted by permission of Fortress Press.

Quotations from *Four Prophets* by J. B. Phillips reprinted by permission of The Macmillan Company.

Quotations from "The Origins of Life" by George Wald in *The Scientific Endeavor* reprinted by permission of The Rockefeller University Press.

Quotations from *The New Testament in the Language of Today* by William Beck reprinted by permission.

Manufactured in the United States of America

Kingdoms of Man
and the
Kingdom of God

To my parents,
who started the thinking
of many of the thoughts
that are in this book

Contents

PREFACE 11

CHAPTER ONE:

WORDS AND MEANINGS 13

CHAPTER TWO:

THE KINGDOMS OF GOD 33

CHAPTER THREE:

THE KINGDOMS OF MEN 57

CHAPTER FOUR:

CHANGE AND DECAY 79

CHAPTER FIVE:

WARS AND RUMORS OF WARS 91

CHAPTER SIX:

EVEN SO, COME 113

ABBREVIATIONS FOR BIBLICAL TRANSLATIONS
USED IN THIS BOOK

ANB — *The Anchor Bible* (Doubleday & Company, Inc., Garden City). Consult volume concerned for translator and date.

Author — *The Psalms in Modern Speech* by Richard S. Hanson (Fortress Press, Philadelphia, 1968). Where an unpublished translation by the author is used, it will be so designated.

Beck — *The New Testament in the Language of Today* by William F. Beck (Concordia Publishing House, St. Louis, 1964).

Phillips — *Four Prophets* by J. B. Phillips (Macmillan, New York, 1963).

RSV — The Revised Standard Version of the Old and New Testaments.

PREFACE

Ours is a time of change, a time of revolution—to such a degree that many live in fear and uncertainty. New ideas threaten old institutions. New moods strain the walls of old wineskins. Old structures that seemed to be permanent are cracking and crumbling, and feelings of pride and security which hinged on their permanency give way to irrational dread. Wars are being fought for no greater reason than fear itself, and nation takes the field against nation in the conviction that rational procedures cannot handle the situations that face us. The easy relief that comes with focusing our fears on others like ourselves tempts us into destructive behavior, while sheer desperation drives some men to uncontrolled violence.

This is the world which surrounds us, and this is the context in which the words of this book are written. We sense the fear of our times and we think that the fear is rooted in confusion. The confusion is about what is real and, therefore, a discussion about what is real may help us to live and endure. We do not seem to be able to distinguish between the significant and the insignificant, the precious and the trite, the permanent and the temporal. In this study we have called it a confusion of kingdoms and assert that it is valuable to know the difference between the kingdoms of men and the Kingdom of God. We believe that knowing the difference will help us to put faith where faith belongs and live with confidence despite all apparent uncertainties. Indeed, we believe that there is as much reason for confidence and hope today as there ever has been, but that confidence and hope depend upon seeing these important distinctions.

We write out of the tradition itself. Because we have found that the words of our sacred Scriptures make the distinctions that are needed and speak with hope out of times that were often like ours, we dare to speak as biblical theologians and quote the words of the past for times that we call today.

Our concern is partly ethical, and the manuscript for this book was first written as a preface to the making of ethical decisions. We know that people are asked to make all sorts of commitments to powers that be and that many of these calls to commitment are in conflict with each other. Life, money, and soul may be demanded by political realities that stand in opposition to each other or to the natural desires that motivate daily living. How does a person decide? To which of the buyers will he sell his soul? We hope that the considerations in this book will in some measure help the reader to make those decisions with good conscience and happy results.

RICHARD S. HANSON

CHAPTER ONE

WORDS AND MEANINGS

Language can serve as well to conceal as to reveal what a person is trying to say. Ordinary words may have different meanings for different people and some words are extraordinarily subject to diverse connotations. To reduce the risk of misunderstanding, we begin our essay with a discussion of three such words: *God, kingdom,* and *world.*

To some, the term *God* denotes anything to do with the conscience. Their God is the voice that speaks the no-no's, whether it concerns such a major issue as the murder of one's wife or such a trite thing as an extra dessert at mealtime. Persons who hold this definition are not particularly fond of their gods (I use the plural because there are many consciences of men), for they are always in the position of being peeked at, scolded, or judged by the constant presence and forced to either rationalize their behavior before it or stick out their tongues in defiance. This concept of God is identified with the parental image, the whole set of early influences that establish our sense for right and wrong and propriety.

It is amusing to behold those whose God is the conscience as they leave the environment in which they were carefully schooled and encounter another human of equal schooling in a different set of mores. They may be college roommates, a country girl dating a boy from Chicago, or two spinsters—each from a different part of the world—teamed up as traveling partners on a tour of the Holy Land. Imagine the shock as one discovers that what his God strictly forbids can be freely and thoroughly enjoyed by the other person. I suppose his first reaction is to think of the other as some godless (i.e., conscienceless) infidel. Then picture the readjustment necessary as the infidel displays piety of a degree that goes beyond that of his judge! What alternative is there but to label the fellow a hypocrite?

Eventually it will have to be recognized that in some areas their two consciences do not agree. This, of course, demands some adjustments of judgment.

(1) Perhaps each man has his own God and we can be happy and friendly if I let you have yours and you allow me mine.

(2) Perhaps this one called God is more tolerant than Mommy and Daddy said. If I watch where the lightning strikes, I may discover which of his rules are inviolable and which can be broken with scarcely any penalty at all.

(3) Perhaps there is no God. If there is supposed to be only one (i.e., One Universal Con-

science), then how can I account for the different commandments by which you live other than to say we have both been fooled. Our mommies and daddies betrayed us. Let's raise hell together and see what happens. If no lightning strikes, there is no God!

This conscience that functions as God can perform at either an individual or a group level. It relies on a stable environment and a cultural heritage for its establishment in the mind of an individual, but once that single person leaves his home culture he can carry that conscience with him and live by it though all the world around him lives by another code. It follows, then, that wherever there is an identifiable group with an understood set of mores, this god is present for any and all who will let him play the role. He is unavailable only to those persons who are tossed to and fro in their formative years, encountering more than one set of codes to test their ability to survive. To such, expediency rather than conscience is apt to be God. The only deity to rule such a person is the biological drive within him—the power that brought him into being and the force that will sustain him until a bullet or the arm of the law brings him down.

There is, of course, a good side to conscience. Good fortune is in store for those who learn the rules and play its game and, if a man is wise enough to figure it all out, the conscience can be an excellent guide to success and prosperity. It can be, in fact, a veritable genie of good fortune.

I have encountered young people whose god was

fundamentally such a genie but whose faith was shattered when they encountered a sizable defeat. One such was an introspective and devout young man whose God had spoken to him in the years of early adolescence and assured him that he was to pursue the calling of medicine and save the world as a pious and devoted physician. All went well for more than three years: he excelled in his high school work, acted as a young man of such serious intentions should act, and heard the approving voices of the adults around him—supporting him with the assurance that he had made a wise choice and was being a most excellent young man in every way. Thus it was until he took a biology course in his first year of college. Biology was not his talent and despite the patience of fine, dedicated teachers, he ended it all with a resounding "D." The young man came to see me in my office and began the description of his spiritual ailment by informing me—in the saddest of tones—that he had lost his faith in God.

I suppose that what we are discussing now is the most private of all the gods men can believe in. It is derived from the great God called conscience but is a very special kind of offspring tailored to the specific needs of the individual saint. Conveniently, the Christian tradition has provided both Father (Conscience) and Son (the friendly Genie) for those of its adherents whose needs reach out for such a pair.

There seem to be a good many to whom the term God is the summation of all past irrelevancies—the famous grandfather with flowing beard who symbolizes the value systems of our ancestors (which must, of course, bow before the realities of our modern age).

This is the God of the funeral parlor and, like it or not, the most irreverent agnostic is apt to pay tribute to him at the death of an elder. Indeed, he will invoke this God's blessing for weddings as well and even condescend to the baptism of his infant offspring in the name of this God without undue pressure from the older generation. We have a good bit of daring before this God in the years of our youth, but once we settle down to rearing our families we grant him a goodly tithe of our religious devotion.

I have often wondered why basically irreverent people should grant this God such a corner of influence. Perhaps it is because of certain mysteries—many of them simple feelings within them—which they find quite baffling. When the patriarchal God is put in charge of those mysteries, a certain peace of mind is gained in return, and it is all worth the little token of support they give the local church in payment for keeping this God alive.

Somewhat fuzzily related to this concept is *God* as applied to all the unexplainable aspects of the realities we confront. Such a "God of the gaps" is used to cope with mysteries that defy human explanation. This is the God who is challenged by "science" and who, because of the steady growth of our world of understanding, diminishes in size each year. As we solve more and more of the puzzles of the universe, less and less do we need this God. When pitted against the growing powers of the reason of man such a God comes out the loser more often than not, for man, after all, is the judge of the tourney.

In the blissful innocence of a prescientific age there

was great need for this God. He was the explanation for sickness, plague, death, and every kind of fortune that could befall us. Now that we know about germs and viruses, however, and now that scientific method has become a common thing, we have few mysteries left to assign to his wisdom. Indeed, the day may come when we have no need for this God at all.

So far all our talk has been about things that people can refer to when they use the term *God*. This reference does not always signify much, for many intend to grant as little power as necessary to God. But ask what is *really* their God and you may be confronted with quite a different set of realities. What is *really* *God* to any person is what he would give his life for if necessary, the recipient of most of his energy and efforts. What is *really God* to a man may be detected at the point where he registers his greatest anxiety and fear. For some it is the source of their daily bread. For others it is whatever supports their own image of themselves. What is *really God* to any person is that which stands for the foundation and basis of his existence, and gives sense and meaning to his life. Yet he may not even refer to that as *God* and for that reason we leave it out of our discussion at this stage.

We use the term *God* in this book in the sense that it is used in biblical literature.

The biblical God is, first and foremost, the creative will that underlies and comprehends all things, the power that brought all into being, and continues to sustain and transform. The opening chapter of Genesis speaks of the life-giving breath or wind (a feminine concept!) that hovered over the abyss of nothing before there was anything else. Its name for God is *Elohim,* the plurality of God, who called forth all realities by speaking the mere intention of their existence. In the prophetic literature it is the majestic Lord of all creatures and men whose formless presence cannot be depicted by any sculptor or artist. He whom the Hebrews worshiped as God was nothing short of the ultimate power of all powers, the force that comprehends everything and is the unity of all we perceive.

The contrast between what is truly God and what is not is described in a number of biblical sources. Psalm 115 is typical of the liturgical literature that speaks on this theme.

> Why should the nations be saying,
>   "Where is your God?"
> when our God is in heaven
> and does whatever he pleases?
>
> Their idols are silver and gold,
>   the work of men's hands,
> with mouths that speak not a word,
> with eyes unable to see,
> with ears that hear not a thing
> and a nose that draws no breath.
> Their hands cannot feel;
> their feet cannot walk;
> their throat cannot growl.
>
> Those who make them are like them
> and so are those who trust them.
>   (vv. 2-8, Author)

Yet none is so articulate at this point as the incomparable Second Isaiah:

Who has measured the waters in the hollow of his hand
and marked off the heavens with a span,
enclosed the dust of the earth in a measure
and weighed the mountains in scales
and the hills in a balance?
Who has directed the Spirit of the Lord,
or as his counselor has instructed him?
Whom did he consult for his enlightenment,
and who taught him the path of justice,
and taught him knowledge,
and showed him the way of understanding?
Behold, the nations are like a drop from a bucket,
and are accounted as the dust on the scales;
behold, he takes up the isles like fine dust.
Lebanon would not suffice for fuel,
nor are its beasts enough for a burnt offering.
All the nations are as nothing before him,
they are accounted by him as less than nothing and emptiness.

To whom then will you liken God,
or what likeness compare with him?
The idol! a workman casts it,
and a goldsmith overlays it with gold,
and casts for it silver chains.
He who is impoverished chooses for an offering
wood that will not rot;
he seeks out a skilful craftsman
to set up an image that will not move.

Have you not known? Have you not heard?
Has it not been told you from the beginning?
Have you not understood from the foundations of the earth?
It is he who sits above the circle of the earth,
and its inhabitants are like grasshoppers;
who stretches out the heavens like a curtain,
and spreads them like a tent to dwell in;
who brings princes to nought,
and makes the rulers of the earth as nothing.

Scarcely are they planted, scarcely sown,
scarcely has their stem taken root in the earth,
when he blows upon them, and they wither,
and the tempest carries them off like stubble.

To whom then will you compare me,
that I should be like him? says the Holy One.
Lift up your eyes on high and see:
   who created these?
He who brings out their host by number,
calling them all by name;
by the greatness of his might,
and because he is strong in power,
not one is missing.

                    (Isa. 40:12-26, RSV)

One of the most subtle contrasts between the true
reality of God and what men settle for short of that
reality is in the Book of Job. There is a conflict between Job and his comforters as they seek to explain
what has befallen the unfortunate man. As the dia-
logue progresses it is obvious that the question goes
beyond immediate causes to the very definition of
God. To the comforters of Job, God is unquestionably
identified with the system of justice they know and
understand to be true. He is the patron power of their
culture, the divine endorsement of the ways they have
learned so well. His "nature" is well summarized in
the first of Bildad's speeches.

       How long will you prate so?
       Your speech is so much wind.
       Does God pervert justice?
       Does Shaddai distort the right?
       Your children sinned against him,
       And he paid them for their sin.

If you will but look to God
And implore the mercy of Shaddai,
If you are pure and upright,
He will bestir himself for you
And restore your righteous estate.
Then your past will be as nothing,
And your future will prosper greatly.
Only ask past generations,
Consider the lore of the patriarchs.
We are ephemeral and know nothing,
For our days on earth are a shadow.
Will they not teach you and tell you,
And bring forth words from their minds?
Can papyrus grow without marsh?
Rushes flourish without water?
While still fresh and uncut,
'Twould wither quicker than grass.
Such is the fate of all who forget God;
The hope of the impious will perish.
His confidence a gossamer thread,
His trust a spider's house.
He leans on his house, it does not stand;
He grasps it, but it will not hold.
Moist is he in the sunlight,
His roots spread over his garden.
Round a rock pile his tendrils twist;
A house of stone they grasp.
When he is swallowed up from his place,
It disowns him: 'I never saw you.'
Lo, this is the joy of his way,
And from the dust another sprouts.
God will not reject the upright,
Nor grasp the hand of evildoers.
He will yet fill your mouth with laughter,
Your lips with shouts of joy.
Your enemies will be clothed with shame.
The tent of the wicked will vanish.

(Job 8, ANB)

At the end of the drama the real God stands up and only Job is willing to listen to him. Appropriate to his identity, he speaks from the vortex of a whirlwind. His dimensions transcend the culture and heritage with which Bildad and company identified him. He turns out to be nothing other than the propounder of puzzles and the sum of all nature's mysteries. He is the one who makes things happen and Job is shown that the unaccountable paradox of his own dilemma is but one sample of a million mysteries of the same sort. When men try to identify God with their logical answers to life's questions, they miss him entirely. He made up the questions and he is the extreme opposite of their ready answers. He is the one whose ways are above our ways, whose thoughts transcend our thoughts, whose majesty is a disturbance to all closed minds.

Here, then, is a sample of the God of Job, of him we shall refer to as God throughout this book.

> Then Yahweh answered Job
> From out of the storm, and said:
> "Who is this that denies Providence
> With words void of knowledge?
> Gird your loins like a hero,
> I will ask you, and you tell me.
> Where were you when I founded the earth?
> Tell me, if you know so much.
> Who drafted its dimensions? Do you know?
> Who stretched the line over it?
> On what are its sockets sunk,
> Who laid its cornerstone,
> While the morning stars sang together,
> And all the gods exulted?

Who shut the sea within doors,
When it came gushing from the womb;
When I made the cloud its garment,
Dark mist its swaddling bands,
When I put bounds upon it,
Set up bars and doors,
Saying, 'Thus far come but no more.
Here your wild waves halt'?
Did you ever command morning,
Post Dawn in his place,
Snatch off Earth's skirts,
Shaking the wicked out of it?
It changes like sealing clay,
Tinted like a garment.
The wicked are robbed of their light,
The upraised arm is broken.
Have you entered the springs of the sea,
Walked in the recesses of the deep?
Have Death's Gates been revealed to you
Have you seen the Dark Portals?
Have you examined earth's expanse?
Tell, if you know all this.
Where is the way to light's dwelling,
Darkness, where its abode,
That you may guide it to its bourne,
Show it the way to go home?
You know, for you were born there,
The sum of your days is great!
Have you entered the snow stores,
Or seen the hoards of hail
Which I reserve for troublous times,
For the day of attack and war?
By what power is the flood divided,
The east [wind] spread over the earth?
Who cleft a channel for the downpour,
A path for the thundershower,
To bring rain on no-man's land,

The wilderness with no man in it,
To sate the desolate desert,
Make the thirsty land sprout verdure?
Does the rain have a father,
Who sired the dew drops?
From whose womb comes the ice,
The hoarfrost of heaven, who bore it,
When water hardens like stone,
The surface of the deep imprisoned?
Can you tie Pleiades' fetters,
Or loose Orion's bands?
Can you lead out Mazzarot on time,
Guide the Bear with her cubs?

(Job 38:1-2, ANB)

When the biblical writers speak of God (and they do so with a remarkable range of vocabulary) they speak of that which comprehends all reality—the familiar together with the unfamiliar—and is the source of that which we do not perceive as well as what we think we understand. He is not to be identified with any system or culture of man nor with anything else that man can create or control. Yet he holds all human systems within his power and may even grant them his blessing. Human words about him are tolerated and necessary, but he is not to be tied to any of those words or their combinations.

The biblical God was the God of the gods of old, holding sway over all powers designated and worshiped as gods by others. Other men recognized this power who reigned supreme over the heavenly council, but only the children of Israel dared worship him. And to worship him was to contend with Something that could not be fooled or flattered, bribed or cajoled.

It was responding to what ultimately controls all things and gives freedom only within limits. The monotheism of the Old Testament was not the introduction of a brand new God into human consciousness. The Power that persuaded Abram to move from Ur was known to the patriarch's neighbors and had names by which he could be called. He was *El—El Shaddai, El Olam, El Elyon*—the president of the pantheon who presided over all other gods but was not worshiped by man directly. The uniqueness of the biblical Hebrews is that they were presumptuous enough to worship the Power that was supreme among the gods. This was a kind of *hubris* or pride not easily tolerated by their culture. Men were to worship the lesser gods. When Abram felt himself called by the God of gods, he succumbed to the most audacious thought that ever tempted a man of old. Abram's God was the most that a god can be and far more than most men can allow.

A second term that might cause some difficulty is *kingdom*. In recent centuries we have seen the appearance of constitutional governments that make the kingdoms of old obsolete and repulsive to us. Since a king was only a benevolent tyrant at best, all kingdoms represent something about humanity we can no longer accept. At one time, however, kingdoms were the only forms of government known above the tribal or city level.

We use the term *kingdom* in this book in its broadest and most universal sense—synonymous with the word *realm*. When we speak of "human kingdoms," then, we do not mean to limit ourselves to organizations headed by kings; and when we refer to "the kingdom of God" we do not mean to suggest that God is any more like a king than anything else—no matter how strikingly that term may denote his functions. In short, we use the term *kingdom* simply because it is traditional and common. We will speak of both human and divine kingdoms, but mostly for the sake of pointing out the distinctions between them.

A third troublesome term is *world*. Its occurrences in English translations of the Bible have long been a source of confusion. There are three senses in which it is used, and a clear understanding of these usages is essential to reading an English version of the Bible with intelligence.

In one category the term is simply a synonym for *earth* and denotes the order created by God. Psalm 24 begins with an excellent illustration of such usage.

> The Lord owns the earth and its contents,
> the world and its creatures.
>
> (Author)

The world thus referred to by ancients was relatively small compared to what lies on our horizons, for great portions of this planet were beyond their view. On the principle that God's place is inaccessible to man, the heavens were excluded and placed in a separate category of their own. That the heavens have now become part of our experience is the simplest sign of how our perception has increased since the days when the biblical books were written. The only way to cope with this change is to allow the term *world* to include more than it did in the past. We can now freely use *universe* in our translations and still carry the basic meaning that this concept had to men of old. To handle any further adjustments that may be necessary, we can say that this usage of the term *world* is meant to designate all that God has created insofar as it is accessible to man's perception.

The term *world* also refers to periods of time—to an era or an age. "To the close of the age" is the RSV rendering of what was once quoted as "unto the end of the world" in Matthew 28:20. "End of the world" is a common liturgical phrase, and to a host of partially educated people this suggests something quite bizarre and foreign to the biblical message. Many, I am sure, envision the crumbling of God's creation. But in the literature of the Scriptures that phrase is used to refer to the close of an era. Jews use the phrase, "world to come," and by it they mean the era that shall dawn after the passing of this one in which we live. They mean a new order, not a new planet. They mean a fulfillment of God's will that makes all past ages look shoddy—yet a perfecting of the very world with which God began in the distant past.

The most unique usage of the term is to be found in John's New Testament writings. John puts "the world" in the anti-God half of his dualism, but he does not mean the creation that is declared good in the first chapter of Genesis. Inasmuch as it is a world characterized by hate, fear, death, and darkness, it is clearly the world of man's own creation, the world of human culture(s). Because of its nature and origin, this world must bend before the power of a more enduring realm and eventually "pass away." "The world" which John pits against God is a world of man's making. More specifically, it consists of those things we create in response to our fears.

We don't have to imagine the distortions produced when men fail to distinguish between these three uses of the term *world,* for our traditions have established some of them as orthodox truth. With roots that go deep into the soil of gnosticism and find their nourishment in nature-negating asceticism, these perversions of the biblical message have grown and borne much poisonous fruit. Some of our Christian teachers have tended to be careless in their observations, too often assuming that "world" must only refer to the planet that is our home. As a result, they are willing to turn the God of the Old Testament into an evil maker of matter—or tolerate an inconsistency that defies the biblical evidence. With unaccountable glee they are willing to proclaim the end and destruction of that which is supposed to be our happy home as long as our Lord sustains us with the gift of life. Such hostility toward the environment can only be accounted for on psychological grounds, and if anything is a sign of our alienation from God, this is it.

Our stated concern results from our perception of a certain fear of change among many people in our culture. There seems to be a frenzied grasping after anything that possesses some semblance of permanence. People are acting as though they have been betrayed by whatever is supposed to be God when they hear of riots and radical new social movements, when they see new political forms gaining ground in the arena of world powers, and when they behold the familiar things of the good old days giving way before new styles and habits. For a while there was a turning to the churches, for they seemed to be bastions of the changeless past. But then the new theologians got out of the seminaries and into the pulpits, and some of the churches began to look like the most dangerous places of all. The hallowed spot where we used to hear about what is the same yesterday and today and forever now sounds like a zoo full of wild mutations fresh from the radiated wombs of atomic victims. Most baffling of all, we hear some saying—as though it were the most sensible thing in all the world—God is dead.

We would be greatly calmed if we could learn to expect certain changes as a matter of course and be shown that the only thing which makes our age more frightening (or exciting!) is an acceleration of its pace. Indeed, we can show how the changeless is best seen in the very process of change itself—that the change and decay on every hand is only a proclamation of the glory of the eternal. To that end we shall make some distinctions between kinds of changes and operate a little like a psychotherapist who gets at healing by first sorting out the tangle of strings that make up the knot of the problem.

We shall try to distinguish between changes that are inevitable (and good) and those that are avoidable (and not necessarily good or bad). Similarly, we shall distinguish between conflict that is part of the "natural order" of things and conflict that is unnecessary or harmful. We shall see, as an example of some evident relationships, that some conflict is produced primarily by a refusal to accept the inevitability of change and, on the other hand, that some changes come about as the direct result of conflict.

CHAPTER TWO

THE KINGDOMS OF GOD

There are no less than three realities which deserve the title, *Kingdom of God*. The first is all creation. By the definition with which we are operating, God is the lord and owner of all things and therefore his kingdom comprises all things. The second reality to which the title can be applied is Israel, which is a special task force of witnesses—a little kingdom within the greater kingdom. In the Old Testament this group is made up of the descendants of a few chosen Semites. In the New Testament it is broadened to include any and all who believe in God as Abraham believed and register as followers of Jesus. The third reality to which we shall apply the title, *Kingdom of God,* is the kingdom that is coming, that is still in evolution, so to speak, as the creative power brings into being a humanity that will function according to the prophetic dream perceived by a select few in the human race. All three can be called kingdoms of God by virtue of the one thing they have in common: they are creations of the Almighty Mover.

It is strange that so many people deal so lightly with the greater kingdom that is God's: the universe in which we live and of which we all form a part. Stranger still, some actually despise this place to the degree that they will sing, "I'm but a stranger here . . . earth is a desert drear . . . heaven is my home" and look with scorn at the fellow creatures whom God has given us as neighbors. Strangest of all, most of these people display their attitudes in the name of a religion they believe is biblically based.

Yet nothing could be clearer in all Scripture than the claim that all things are God's and all creatures part of his realm. "The Lord owns the earth and its contents," sang the author of Psalm 24, "the world and its creatures." And he sounds the keynote for dozens of doxologies on the same theme.

> Praise The Lord!
> Praise The Lord from the heavens!
> Praise him in the heights!
> Praise him, all his messengers!
> Praise him, all his armies!
> Praise him, sun and moon!
> Praise him, all shining stars!
> Praise him, O heavens beyond heavens,
> O waters above all the heavens!
> Give praise to the name of the Lord!
> At his command you were made.
>
> He made them immovable forever;
> he decreed that they should remain.
>
> Give praise to The Lord from the earth,
> O monsters and all powers of chaos!
> —lightning and storm, snow and clouds,

hot desert wind which blows at his word,
mountains and all high hills,
fruit-bearing trees and cedars,
wild creature and very large beast,
reptile and bird on the wing,
kings of the earth and all peoples,
princes and all of Earth's leaders,
healthy young men and maidens,
old men and children!

Let them all praise the name of The Lord,
his unique, inaccessible name!
His glory covers Earth and Heaven.
He has lifted strength from his people,
a hymn of praise from his saints,
from Israel, the people who are near him.
Praise The Lord!

(Psalm 148, Author)

Bless The Lord, O my soul!
O Lord, my God, you are great
You are clothed in splendor and glory,
wearing the light as a cloak,
stretching Heaven like a tent.

He covers his chambers with water,
using the clouds as his chariot,
walking on the wings of the wind,
making the winds his messengers
and bolts of fire his servants.
He planted the earth on its moorings,
never again to be moved.

Chaos enshrouded like a cloak;
water stood higher than mountains,
but at your rebuke they fled;
at the sound of your thunder they ran.
The hills rose, the valleys sank down

to the points which you had decreed.
You set the immovable bounds
which protect the earth from the sea.

He puts the springs in the brooks
and they flow between the hills,
watering the life of the meadows,
quenching the thirst of wild beasts.
Overhead dwell the birds of the air,
warbling among the branches.

As you water the hills from above
you satisfy Earth with your produce,
bringing forth grass for the cattle,
vegetation for man to till
to make the earth produce bread.

He makes man happy with wine,
which brightens the face more than oil,
and sustains man's life with bread.

He even provides for his trees,
for the cedars he planted in Lebanon,
the place where the birds build nests,
the trees where the stork has her home.
High mountains are for the wild goats;
the rocks are the lair of the rabbit.
He made the moon to set months,
the sun for its daily journey.

You bring the dark: it is night
and the beasts of the brush creep forth.
The young lions growl at their prey
as they seek their food from God,
but at sunrise they all slink away
to crouch for sleep in their dens.
Then mankind appears for his work,
to work at his tasks until evening.

How numerous are your deeds, O Lord
—and all of them done with such wisdom!
your activity fills the earth.
There is the sea, great and wide,
teeming with innumerable creatures,
large ones and small ones together!
There also the ships journey forth,
where you made the sea monsters to sport.
They all depend upon you
to give them their food in due time.
You give it, for they do but gather.
You open your hand: they have plenty.
You withhold your presence: they are anxious.
You take their breath and they die
and go back to the dust they came from.
Yet you send back the breath and create,
renewing the face of the earth.

May the honor of The Lord endure!
May The Lord rejoice as he works!
He looks on the earth and it trembles.
When he touches the mountains they smoke.
(Ps. 104:1-32, Author)

This greater kingdom of God has one binding force
that ties all its members together: the creator who is
its master. This is the bond that binds every man to his
fellow human, to the other creatures who share his
environment and to the elements around him. For all
these there is one common Lord. And this is no matter
of choice. It is pointless to ask an ostrich, a bee or an
octopus, *or a human being,* "What God created you?"
There is only one force which created all and it remains God whether or not it is acknowledged as such.
Our births are declarations of his creative power and
our deaths are signs of his sovereign authority. No

man can escape being a citizen of this kingdom of God. He is in it by virtue of what he is. Even though he renounce that by committing suicide, other forms of life will claim his remains and adapt them to the service of the creating master.

This kingdom is a kingdom of grace. It is, as Job discovered it to be, a kingdom whose laws are beyond human comprehension, a realm where misfortune can strike any man and a world where sunshine and rain are given to the evil as well as the good. It is a kingdom of grace, for in it all rely on the gracious giving of the Lord who creates, sustains, and transforms. It is a kingdom of grace, for we see that

> the race is not to the swift
> nor the battle to the mighty
> —nor even wealth to the clever
> or favor to the learned,
> for time and chance befall them all.
>
> (Eccles. 9:11, Author, unpublished)

Man cannot make this kingdom conform to his desires except within limits that are hard to determine. In fact, his survival hinges very much on his willingness to submit to what appears to be an element of caprice in its laws.

This is the kingdom that endures, the world that was made "immovable forever." Within it the grass may wither, the flower may fade, and man, like the grass and flowers, go back to the dust he came from, but over-riding every cycle of growth and decay is the life-producing principle that goes on. The source and sustenance of the kingdom is eternal; it does not pass away. There is no better simile for it than the mustard seed or the yeast in bread, for the mystery of life that is hidden there is the essence of the power that generates and sustains that kingdom.

The biblical writings also speak of a little kingdom within God's greater realm, selected for the sake of a crucial mission. Its constitution is given in Exodus 19:1-6 (with repetitions in many more places).

> On the third new moon after the Israelites had gone forth from the land of Egypt, on that very day, they entered the wilderness of Sinai. Having journeyed from Rephidim, they entered the wilderness of Sinai and encamped in the wilderness. Israel encamped there in front of the mountain, and Moses went up to God. The LORD called to him from the mountain, saying, "Thus shall you say to the house of Jacob and declare to the children of Israel: 'You have seen what I did to the Egyptians, how I bore you on eagles' wings and brought you to Me. Now then, if you will obey Me faithfully and keep My covenant, you shall be My treasured possession among all the peoples. Indeed, all the earth is Mine, but you shall be to Me a kingdom of priests and a holy nation.' These are the words that you shall speak to the children of Israel."

(Author, unpublished)

This kingdom was called into being to declare the reality of God and his sovereignty before all men. Its vocation was to live and to die in testimony to the glory of earth's Creator, to show other men the possibility of worshiping something beyond the immediate powers of their environment, higher than their own powers of reason. It was not to think of itself as God's only kingdom ("all the earth is mine") but as a people with a special vocation, called to be a blessing to the world.

> Bring forth the people who are blind, yet have eyes,
>   who are deaf, yet have ears!
> Let all the nations gather together,
>   and let the peoples assemble.
> Who among them can declare this,
>   and show us the former things?
> Let them bring their witnesses to justify them,
>   and let them hear and say, It is true.
> *"You are my witnesses,"* says the LORD,
>   "and my servant whom I have chosen,
> that you may know and believe me
>   and understand that I am He.
> Before me no god was formed,
>   nor shall there be any after me.
> I, I am the LORD,
>   and besides me there is no savior.
> I declared and saved and proclaimed,
>   where there was no strange god among you;
>   and you are my witnesses," says the LORD.
>   (Isa. 43:8-12, RSV, my italics)

> Thus says the LORD, the King of Israel
> and his Redeemer, the LORD of hosts:
> "I am the first and I am the last;
>   besides me there is no god.
> Who is like me? Let him proclaim it,
>   let him declare and set it forth before me.
> Who has announced from of old the things to come?
>   Let them tell us what is yet to be.
> Fear not, nor be afraid;
>   have I not told you from of old and declared it?
>   And *you are my witnesses!*
> Is there a God besides me?
>   There is no Rock; I know not any."
>   (Isa. 44:6-8, RSV, my italics)

Israel was God's creation. Like the world around her, she sprang forth in response to a word from God and took shape—a testimony to the continuing creative power of God. In her history—her tragedies and triumphs—the world is to see, in miniature, the acts of God that surround them in the greater kingdom to which they all belong. "Then you shall know that I am Yahweh (he who brings into being)": this is the recurring theme of the Book of Ezekiel and the prophet is speaking of Israel's travails and future glory. Israel is the bearer of God's honor and, as her prayers and hymns mount to the winds, that honor is given its glory.

> You are the Holy One,
> throned on the praises of Israel.
> Our fathers believed in you;
> they trusted and you set them free.
> They cried unto you and you freed them;
> they hoped and were not disappointed.
> (Ps. 22:4-6, Author)

Not that Israel lived up to her task all that well. Her prophets chastised her again and again for her failures.

> Sons have I reared and brought up,
> but they have rebelled against me.
> The ox knows its owner,
> and the ass its master's crib;
> but Israel does not know,
> my people does not understand.
> (Isa. 1:2-3, RSV)

> For cross to the coasts of Cyprus and see,
> or send to Kedar and examine with care;

see if there has been such a thing.
Has a nation changed its gods,
   even though they are no gods?
But my people have changed their glory
   for that which does not profit.
Be appalled, O heavens, at this,
be shocked, be utterly desolate, says the LORD,
for my people have committed two evils:
they have forsaken me,
the fountain of living waters,
and hewed out cisterns for themselves,
broken cisterns, that can hold no water.

(Jer. 2:10-13, RSV)

Israel's calling was to "know" the God who is Lord of all men and proclaim that knowledge before them. As a summation of the whole prophetic indictment an ancient author created the story of Jonah, who is Israel surviving her own failures. She could never quite believe in her calling and yet she could not escape it. Every failure only cursed her to redemption and another chance. The belly of the fish could not hold her, for it was God's will to see her task fulfilled despite her reticence and weakness. This is the puzzle faced by the apostle Paul as he wonders why the majority of his Jewish contemporaries could not recognize the messianic claims about Jesus and heed the signs of the times. Like the anonymous author of Jonah, he sees that their rejection can never induce God to leave them.

The New Testament is the announcement that God's little kingdom of witnesses is now to be enlarged. An era has come to an end and a new age is dawning. God will no longer restrict himself to a

certain ethnic group. The time has come for a new
Israel to be formed out of men and women from
every tribe and nation. The distinction between Jew
and Greek has ended. All who will heed the proclamation of Jesus as the long-awaited King of the Jews and
the fulfillment—in person—of the old Israel's vocation
are valid members of this new reality. As Peter states
it (in a deliberate recasting of passages from Exodus
19 and Hosea), a new Israel has come into being.

> But you are a chosen people, priests of a King, a holy
> nation, a people saved to be His own and to tell of
> the wonderful deeds of Him who called you out of
> darkness into His marvelous light. Once you were
> no people, but now you are God's people. Once you
> had received no mercy, but now you have received
> mercy.
>
> (I Peter 2:9-10, Beck)

The Gospel according to Mark captures the spirit
of fulfilled expectations as it tells the story of one who
spoke with authority, successfully challenging both the
rigid religious establishment and the demons which
oppressed his people. The Gospel according to Luke
describes the ministry of this man as God at work
"scattering the proud" and "helping his servant Israel"
—one anointed

> to preach good news to the poor
> ... to proclaim release to the captives
> and recovery of sight to the blind,
> to free those who are oppressed,
> to proclaim the favorable [*dekton*] year of the Lord.
>
> (Luke 4:18, quoting Isa. 61:1-2;
> translation by Beck)

The Gospel according to Matthew is a studied attempt to portray Jesus as the fulfillment of Israel's vocation, the Moses-figure who ushers in the era of New Israel with a new Torah appropriate to the occasion. From beginning to end, the New Testament announces the turning of an age, the beginning of the premessianic era. Israel's messiah has appeared and can now be proclaimed to the nations in preparation for his lordship over all.

Not that this was the first attempt at such a message. The exciting advent of the Persian empire led the Second Isaiah to announce that Cyrus was God's messiah (Isa. 45:1 ff.) and to see the possibility of such an age centuries before Jesus of Nazareth. Moreover, that prophet's disciples were willing to admit the gentiles into God's kingdom of Israel even at that time.

> Let not the foreigner who has joined
>   himself to the Lord say,
>   "The Lord will surely separate me from his people";
>   ... the foreigners who join themselves to the Lord,
> to minister to him, to love the name of the Lord,
>   and to be his servants,
> every one who keeps the sabbath,
>   and does not profane it,
>   and holds fast my covenant—
> these I will bring to my holy mountain
> and make them joyful in my house of prayer;
> their burnt offerings and their sacrifices
>   will be accepted on my altar;
> for my house shall be called a house of prayer
>   for all peoples.
> Thus says the Lord God,
>   who gathers the outcasts of Israel,

I will gather yet others to him
  besides those already gathered."

(Isa. 56:3-8, RSV)

Arise, shine; for your light has come,
and the glory of the LORD has risen upon you.
For behold, darkness shall cover the earth,
  and thick darkness the peoples;
but the LORD will arise upon you,
and his glory will be seen upon you.
And nations shall come to your light,
and kings to the brightness of your rising.

Lift up your eyes round about, and see;
they all gather together, they come to you;
your sons shall come from far,
and your daughters shall be carried in the arms.
Then you shall see and be radiant,
your heart shall thrill and rejoice;
because the abundance of the sea
  shall be turned to you,
the wealth of the nations shall come to you.
A multitude of camels shall cover you,
  the young camels of Midian and Ephah;
  all those from Sheba shall come.
They shall bring gold and frankincense,
  and shall proclaim the praise of the LORD.
All the flocks of Kedar shall be gathered to you,
the rams of Nebaioth shall minister to you;
they shall come up with acceptance on my altar,
and I will glorify my glorious house.

(Isa. 60:1-7, RSV)

Following in that train came the one who rewrote
the story of Ruth to point out the non-Jewish blood in
the royal line of David and the gifted author of Jonah
who believed in the possibility of "Nineveh's" repen-

tance if Israel would but exercise her prophetic mission. (Nineveh was a symbol for the mightiest and fiercest of the heathen.)

Inextricably entwined with the notion of God's selection of Israel for a prophetic mission is the idea of a Jewish king whose throne is the seat of God's own sovereign power. This claim was not recognized by all the sons of Israel (see 1 Kings 12) but those who believed it saw so much in the office that they asserted his royal sovereignty over other nations as well as their own. He was more than king of Judah or even Judah-Israel (see Ezek. 37:15-28 and similar passages in Isaiah and Jeremiah). He was the signet ring of God's authority over his larger kingdom as well.

> The word of the LORD came a second time to Haggai on the twenty-fourth day of the month, "Speak to Zerubbabel, governor of Judah, saying, I am about to shake the heavens and the earth, and to overthrow the throne of kingdoms; I am about to destroy the strength of the kingdoms of the nations, and overthrow the chariots and their riders; and the horses and their riders shall go down, every one by the sword of his fellow. On that day, says the LORD of hosts, I will take you, O Zerubbabel my servant, the son of Shealtiel, says the LORD, and make you like a signet ring; for I have chosen you, says the LORD of hosts."
>
> (Hag. 2:20-23, RSV)

> Rejoice greatly, O daughter of Zion!
> Shout aloud, O daughter of Jerusalem!
> Lo, your king comes to you;
>   triumphant and victorious is he,
> humble and riding on an ass,

on a colt the foal of an ass.
I will cut off the chariot from Ephraim
and the war horse from Jerusalem;
and the battle bow shall be cut off,
and he shall command peace to the nations;
his dominion shall be from sea to sea,
from the River to the ends of the earth.

(Zech. 9:9-10, RSV, my italics)

O God, give your justice to the king,
your righteousness to the prince,
that he rule your people correctly,
your needy ones justly!
May the hills produce peace for the people,
the mountains bring victory!
May he plead for the needy,
give help to the poor
and crush the oppressor!

Descend, O rain, on the grass,
O showers that soak the land!
Make his days fruitful, O Righteous One!
Increase the yearly prosperity.
May he rule from sea unto sea,
from the River to the ends of the earth!
May the sea countries bow before him!
May his enemies grovel in the dust!
May the kings of Tarshish and Greece bring him a gift!
May the kings of Sheba and Seba draw near with tribute!
May all the kings bow before him!
May all the nations serve him!

(Ps. 72:1-11, Author)

When the New Testament makes its messianic
claims about Jesus of Nazareth it shows him as one
worthy of such universal lordship on several counts.
First, he was not purely Jewish in his outlook. To be

sure, "he came to his own," but he did not share their nationalistic notions and demonstrated, instead, that their national identity must subordinate itself to a greater cause—that they must die for the world if they are to become the world's life, hope, and salvation. His death was intended to be the death of the pride that held them back from performing their mission. His death was to free them for their missionary task. Regardless of how he said it, his disciples understood their job to be the proclamation of his "authority in heaven and earth" among the nations.

This is a profound and weighty claim, not understood by most Christians and overlooked by contemporary Jews. The messianic claims of Jesus rest on two foundation supports of equal importance: (1) his intentional identity with his own heritage and people, and (2) the permission granted his disciples to proclaim him as universal Christ following the fulfillment of that identification.

The crux of it all was Jesus' insistence on suffering and dying in order to rise. The Jewish people had succeeded in putting their messiah in a special category which exempted him from suffering. He could be all things representing the authority of God and the Age to Come, but he could not be the suffering servant. Many of the Jews had so exalted the role of their messiah that they could not accept the humanization of that role as it was played by Jesus. When Jesus announced that it was necessary for the Son of Man to suffer in order to achieve his glory, he was asserting the complete identity of the messiah with his suffering people. In effect, he was saying this: *any messiah who*

*is to be worthy of the office must so share the life and
trials of his people that he joins them in the belly of
the fish.* Having said that, he committed himself to
the path that led to his triumph. But this was unaccept-
able to many of those who had previously followed
him. A messiah who represents God: yes. A messiah
who stands—and falls—for the people: no. It was
Jesus' prophetic understanding of the messianic role
that caused his first loss of followers and even made
Peter resist him.

The evangelist Luke tried to emphasize the universal
aspect of Jesus' mission by bringing into the picture
every gentile he could find. This might not have been
necessary, for Jesus could have been proclaimed universal Lord even if he had restricted himself to serving the
Jews alone. Had he but fulfilled what a messiah should
be *for them,* he would free them and the messianic
office to be for all men. Indeed, his first task was to
transform his own people into what they ought to be.
Only then could they be the prophetic people they
were called to be. Fortunately, a handful of first-
century Jews understood this and carried his mission
to the next stage of fulfillment.

The anonymous writer of the Letter to the Hebrews
seems to have understood the full scope and implica-
tion of Jesus' messiahship as well as any of the early
theologians. In his view, a change of calendar was in
order. The old age had been brought to fulfillment by
this Jesus who was proclaimed as messiah. This Jew,
he explained, took the first step into the era of a new
covenant that calls for the same kind of endurance
and hope that characterized the faithful saints in the

era of the old covenant—and this new era was the one preceding the final denouement. The messiah who brought Israel's era to a close is the revelation of the eternal. This was the root of his claim to universal power: the fact that he represents the Universal Lord.

And this is the hinge that links us to the third application of the phrase *Kingdom of God:* its use to describe what is happening in all of life and history.

Since the Israelites claimed to worship the God of heaven—the universal God, the president of the council—they also had to claim universal lordship for their messiah. When this God "chose" a descendant of David to be king over Israel, that poor son of David carried a weight of authority greater than any of those who were called gods by the nations.

No other nation could assert such bold claims about its kings—regardless of their genius and power—without speaking a blatant lie. Indeed, when their kings did exalt themselves, their claims were couched in carefully guarded language. Nebuchadrezzar could be the great king only in the name of Marduk (Babylon's patron deity) and Marduk, in turn, could be granted an increase in stature only by a decree from the God who presided above the heavenly court of gods—the one whom the Israelites actually worshiped! So also with the Assyrian kings. Their greatness depended on the greatness of "Lord Assur" and the Assyrian theologians accommodated their theologies to political reality by presenting Assur as one who usurped his lordly position among the gods.

We must note carefully the difference between these imperial claims and what seem to be extravagant claims for the Jewish messiah. When the domain of the Son of David is described as extending "to the ends of the earth," it is in no way a claim to superior power on the part of Judah. It simply asserts that what he represents has a legitimate claim over all men by right of ownership.

The sauciness of this assertion is seen most clearly in the seventh chapter of the Book of Daniel, where the pompous lord of Syria and all other powers of earth must bow before the humble son of man.

> I saw in the night visions,
> and behold, with the clouds of heaven
>   there came one like a son of man,
> and he came to the Ancient of Days
>   and was presented before him.
> And to him was given dominion and glory and kingdom,
> that all peoples, nations, and languages should serve him;
> his dominion is an everlasting dominion,
>   which shall not pass away
> and his kingdom one that shall not be destroyed.
>   (Dan. 7:13-14, RSV)

What is this kingdom that shall be everlasting? It is the kingdom that is in the process of becoming as the kingdoms of men give way to the sway of God's power. This is the key to the biblical interpretation of world history and the clue to what human life is all about. It is the assertion that God's creative acts are not ended, that the "Sabbath rest" of the seventh day is still in the making as he performs his miracles on the unfinished portion of his creation: man.

Among the few of our age who glimpse this is the scientist-theologian, Teilhard de Chardin, who speaks of a process of "divinisation" or "unitive transformation" in which men move to a fulfillment of what humanity was intended to share and to be—a process of being gathered into unity by the creative power which penetrates us from within. He, more than any other, perceives the mystery of the mystical Christ of the apostle Paul: the Christ who can be spoken of as head of a body in which all things are re-united. The Christ who, from the beginning, was in all things. The Christ who comes to gather God's children that all may be one.

The Hasidic mystics of Jewish tradition sometimes describe this happening of history as a drawing together of the sparks into which the Creator diffused his glory by the process of creation. It is as though the Creator tore himself apart in creating for the very sake of embracing and drawing together all created wonders into the wonder of ultimate unity. Yet not just a drawing-together, but a drawing-together that frees or redeems us and all creation to realize the perfection that was planned from the beginning. In contrast to the notion of a perfect-world-gone-to-pot-and-in-need-of-repair, we meet here the notion of a deliberate risk for the sake of greater achievement: God daring dispersion for the sake of creating unity. Martin Buber, a modern apostle of Hasidic ideas, spoke of it as the "unity of becoming" and saw man as God's partner in the unfinished work of creation. For him, the essence of the kingdom to come and the process in which it comes is the realization of community.

The early Christian eucharistic prayer had something of this same thought in it. The telltale words are these: *as this broken bread was scattered upon the mountains and, in being gathered together became one, so may your church be gathered together from the ends of the earth into your kingdom.* The kingdom of God that is spoken of here is the unity and the peace and the glory that shall be when God's will has been done among us as it is in the realms beyond us. This is the hope that was the very life of the early Christian communities, whose capstone prayer was *maranatha*—"our Lord come!"

Yet, if we seek words that first define this kingdom, we must go to the oracles of the Hebrew prophets who preceded those early Christians. The hymnic oracle found in both Micah and Isaiah captures the vision.

In the last days it will come to pass
That the mountain of the Lord
Shall tower above the peaks,
Lifted high above the hills,
And peoples shall swarm to it!
Great nations will arrive and say,
Come, let us go up to the mountain of the Lord,
And to the house of the God of Jacob.
He will give us knowledge of his ways,
And we will follow in his paths.
For the Law goes forth from Zion,
And the Word of the Lord from Jerusalem.
And he will judge between great peoples,
And make decision between nations far and wide.
Then they shall hammer their swords into ploughshares,
And their spears into pruning-hooks.
Nations shall lift no sword against nation,
And never again will they learn to make war.

Every man shall live beneath the shade of his
　　own vine and fig-tree.
And no one shall make him afraid.
The Lord of hosts has declared this with his own voice!

(Mic. 4:1-4, Phillips)

The "end" of all things is the fulfillment of what the
Hebrews called "peace" *(shalom)*, which is not only
the absence of war but the presence of brotherly behavior and the enjoyment of the fruits of the earth.

In the New Testament the vision seems to have
been caught best by John, who saw it as the full realization of God's power in the realm of human existence, the establishment of a fellowship *(koinonia)*
among men and the permeating presence of the force
called *agape* which when acted out ("perfected"),
drives out the fear that resists the coming of this kingdom.

In the Revelation of St. John we find the prophetic
and apocalyptic language of the Old Testament applied to the situation that prevailed under the em-
peror Domitian and in the midst of its triumphant
visions we find this description of the third type of
kingdom.

> Then I saw a new heaven and a new earth, be-
> cause the first heaven and the first earth had passed
> away. And there was no longer any sea. And I saw
> the holy city, a new Jerusalem, coming down from
> God in heaven, dressed as a bride, ready to meet her
> husband.
>
> And I heard a loud voice from the throne say:
> "Look! God's home is among the people, and He
> will live with them. They will be His people, and

God Himself will be with them. He will wipe
every tear from their eyes. There will be no more
grief or crying or pain, because the first things have
passed away."

"Look! I am making everything new," said He
who sat on the throne. And he added, "Write this
because these words are true and you can trust them."
Then He said to me, "It is done! I am A and Z, the
Beginning and the End. To anyone who is thirsty
I will give water that costs nothing, from the spring
of the water of life. Be victorious and you will have
these things, and I will be your God, and you will
be My son."

(Rev. 21:1-7, Beck)

The relationships between the three kingdoms of
God we have been referring to would seem to be as
follows. The first is the reality that is—whether men
acknowledge it or not. The last is the reality that is
taking place as God completes his creative work with
man, the creature who is being made "in his image."
The second kingdom exists for the sake of bringing
about the third.

Yet, despite all distinctions which must be made
for the sake of discussion and understanding, all three
kingdoms are very much the same.

CHAPTER THREE

THE KINGDOMS OF MEN

Listen to this, all peoples!
Give ear, all citizens of Earth!
Men both common and noble,
the rich and the poor together!
My mouth will utter wise things;
the thoughts of my mind are instructive.
I will tune my ear for a lesson
and expose my homily with a harp.

Why should I fear days of trouble,
when the evil of the greedy surrounds me
—of those who trust in their power
and boast of tremendous wealth?

Lo, a man cannot ransom himself.
He cannot pay his money to God
and the price of his life is too high.
Though he wear himself out and live over,
will he not, in the end, see the grave?
He must see that wise men will die;
they shall perish along with the fools
and leave what they earned for others.

Their eternal home is the grave,
their dwelling for all generations
even though they called countries their own.

The splendor of man cannot last:
he is just like the beasts, who perish.
This is the fate of the wealthy,
the last reward of the glutton.
Like sheep, they are numbered for Deathland;
death is the shepherd who rules them.

But God can ransom my life
and release me from Deathland's grasp.
Fear not when a man becomes rich,
when the wealth of his house increases.
When he dies he takes nothing along:
his glory will not descend with him.

His life may be blest while living.
They may praise you for all your good fortune,
but, gone to the realm of your fathers,
you will never again see the light.
Man, in his splendor, knows nothing;
he is just like the beasts, who perish.

                              (Psalm 49, Author)

Our creator has so endowed us that we are all builders of kingdoms from an early age. For some, whose thirst for power is great, the kingdoms must be large and involve the ordering around of other people. For others, a workbench or a kitchen is a realm of sufficient size. There are the defeated, who have given up trying for lack of success, but catch any of us before we are beaten and we all have a measure of this urge.

Place a child in a sandbox and he will so mold the

elements before him that they are transformed into a kingdom of his making. There will be structures and roads, gadgets, and persons to be ordered about, and a detailed program of activities carried out at the behest of the little master. He will speak words, and things will come into being. He will give commands, and there will be happenings.

Put a group of children together and they will organize themselves into leaders and followers, workers and dreamers. There will be, in fact, a loosely-knit sort of government in which rank and authority are carefully observed.

"A man's home is his castle," we say, and that is no trite observation. As surely as a man takes a wife and has children, he (or she!) builds a kingdom with himself as king. Every farm, every business enterprise, every institution of learning, every industrial corporation, every city, every state, is a kingdom of sorts. We are incurable builders of kingdoms.

All this can be stated theologically by saying, "God created us in his own image," for the biblical definition of the phrase, *image of God,* is this: "to subdue and have dominion." God lets us build kingdoms of our own, we can say. The world is his, for he made it, but he made it to be our sandbox. He gave us the mandate to rule it. It is stated most beautifully in Psalm 8, where the Mesopotamian concept of the stars as rulers of earth is challenged with this profound insight.

Lord, our Master,
how powerful your presence on Earth!
Your praise is echoed through the sky.
From the mouths of babes and infants

you have called forth strength despite foes,
silencing enemies and avengers.

When I look at your heavens, the work of your fingers,
the moon and the stars which you have created,
why should you notice a human?
Why should you make use of man?
You have made him almost like God
and crowned him with glory and honor.
You gave him command of your works;
you have placed it all at his feet
—the sheep, the oxen, all of them,
yes, even the beasts of the field,
the birds in the sky, the fish in the sea,
swimming the paths of the ocean.

Lord, our Master,
how powerful your presence on Earth!

(Author)

The only tragic element of this delightful game is
that our kingdoms do not last. Only the kingdom
which is created by him who is eternal can be forever.
The kingdoms made by human hands only illustrate
the mortality of their makers.

My son builds a kingdom of blocks and toy soldiers.
It is a grandly organized affair and his parents must
often agree that "it is a shame to tear it down." But
for the sake of order and neatness in the greater kingdom we call the Hanson houschold, his little kingdom must go. Come bedtime, it is dismantled and its
parts return to the chaos of the toybox. But we do him
no disservice in ordaining this fate. Had we left it up,
his interest might be gone by morning and it would
only stand as a neglected monument to yesterday's fun.

The truth is, he enjoyed building it far more than he could enjoy keeping it safe from harm. By taking it down we encourage him to do it all over—in a different way if he pleases—and permit him to have the fun of building again.

Perhaps this is a worthwhile axiom: it is the building, rather than the ownership, which provides the greater thrill. Humans are meant to build kingdoms, but when they turn to perpetuating their creations, they commit a grave error. It is wrong to try to make something permanent out of that which is meant to last for a day, to make a kingdom of God out of a human affair.

A man and a woman perform the rituals of that ancient mystery called marriage and establish themselves a home. They erect structures to declare its boundaries, protect it from their enemies by a series of insurance policies and retirement plans, procure and arrange furnishings for the sake of their comforts and tastes, and have babies to serve as subjects. For the first several years of their marriage they labor and sweat to build this idyllic realm. Then comes a crucial point in their lives.

If they are wise, they will turn their energies and skills to the building of other kinds of kingdoms and recapture the thrill of that which we have come to associate with youth despite their ripeness of age. If they are not so wise, they will settle down to the business of possessing the kingdom they have built and become like little children screaming when the blocks of a three-day-old toy castle are jostled by someone going about his business. They will become obsessed with "keeping things in place" and "preserving the beauty" of what once was.

Worse than that, they will find that their urge to build has not left them. They will find themselves intruding on the lives of their offspring in order to have a share in the building of their private kingdoms. Forgetting what gave them the real pleasures of their youth, they will deny their own children the right and privilege of kingdom building by "making things easier" for them. "We don't want you to have it as hard as we had it," they will say, but it is really a cover-up for gross selfishness that wants to live life over even if it means denying the essence of human life to one's own son or daughter. Birds are practicing an essential kind of wisdom when they push their young out of the nest and force them to fly. The middle generation of unchallenged Americans should learn from the birds, for then their children might not have to do such extreme and foolish things to protect themselves from the hovering presence of their parents.

I have talked with more than one young person whose basic problem is parents who want to be God. The burden placed on them is unreasonable. They have to choose between the God-given urge to build a kingdom of their own, on the one hand, and their affection and respect for their parents on the other. What an impossible choice! No wonder the youth must escape. Parents who cannot keep their fingers off this sacred process of bringing something new into being ought to be mercifully removed from the scene for awhile, for if they remain and pursue this demonic occupation they will not only ruin the lives of their

children, but they will also lose all the respect and
honor they ever deserved and spend their final days
as disgruntled old cranks mumbling about the dis-
respectful attitude of the younger generation.

According to the Scriptures it was the Lord of Life
himself who said, "Hence a man leaves his father and
mother and clings to his wife. . . ." To say it un-
scripturally: the whole business of pulling away from
the parental ties is a natural principle that ought not
be denied.

There are human kingdoms that can outlast the life-
times of those who create them—business ventures,
farms, corporations, villages, cities, and the like. In
fact, some of them grow to such proportions that they
may last for centuries and *seem* to be eternal. What,
after all, is eternal? It is that which was there when
you were born and which will remain there when you
die. Banking houses and royal families fell into that
category in medieval days. Today the list includes
banking houses, governments, and industrial giants
like General Motors or A. T. & T. These are the
greatest human kingdoms—greatest in size and lon-
gevity—and because they are the greatest, they are the
kingdoms that most seriously challenge the kingdom
of God.

Every kingdom has its king and there is nothing
bad about that so long as the king knows the limits of
his power. (That is the gist of the Deuteronomic
torah about kings as recorded in Deut. 17:14-20.) It is
when the power is extended beyond its natural limits
that offenses occur.

Human kingdoms are supposed to perish. If they do not, they only become traps for posterity. They become false gods that must either be served or destroyed (and *you* may decide which of these two tasks is the least onerous and painful!).

The process of human kingdom-building was well understood by the prophet Ezekiel. So also was the process by which such kingdoms come to nought. His description of the rise and fall of the Phoenician commercial power, Tyre, is most instructive.

The word of the LORD came to me: "Now you, son of man, raise a lamentation over Tyre, and say to Tyre, who dwells at the entrance to the sea, merchant of the peoples on many coastlands, thus says the Lord GOD:

> "O Tyre, you have said,
>   'I am perfect in beauty.'
> Your borders are in the heart of the seas;
>   your builders made perfect your beauty.
> They made all your planks of fir trees from Senir;
>   they took a cedar from Lebanon to make a mast for you.
> Of oaks of Bashan they made your oars;
>   they made your deck of pines from the coasts of Cyprus,
>   inlaid with ivory.
> Of fine embroidered linen from Egypt was your sail,
>   serving as your ensign;
> blue and purple from the coasts of Elishah was your
>   awning.
> The inhabitants of Sidon and Arvad were your rowers;
> skilled men of Zemer were in you;
>   they were your pilots.
> The elders of Gebal and her skilled men were in you,
>   caulking your seams;
> all the ships of the sea with their mariners were in you,
>   to barter for your wares.

"Persia and Lud and Put were in your army as your men of way; they hung the shield and helmet in you; they gave you splendor. The men of Arvad and Helech were upon your walls round about, and men of Gamad were in your towers; they hung their shields upon your walls round about; they made perfect your beauty.

"Tarshish trafficked with you because of your great wealth of every kind; silver, iron, tin, and lead they exchanged for your wares. Javan, Tubal and Meshech traded with you; they exchanged the persons of men and vessels of bronze for your merchandise. Beth-togarmah exchanged for your wares horses, war horses, and mules. The men of Rhodes traded with you; many coastlands were your own special markets; they brought you in payment ivory tusks and ebony. Edom trafficked with you because of your abundant goods; they exchanged for your wares emeralds, purple, embroidered work, fine linen, coral, and agate. Judah and the land of Israel traded with you; they exchanged for your merchandise wheat, olives and early figs, honey, oil and balm. Damascus trafficked with you for your abundant goods, because of your great wealth of every kind: wine of Helbon, and white wool, and wine from Uzal they exchanged for your wares; wrought iron, cassia, and calamas were bartered for your merchandise. Dedan traded with you in saddlecloths for riding. Arabia and all the princes of Kedar were your favored dealers in lambs, rams, and goats; in these they trafficked with you. The traders of Sheba and Raamah traded with you; they exchanged for your wares the best of all kinds of spices, and all precious stones, and gold. Haran, Canneh, Eden, Asshur, and Chilmad traded with you. These traded with you in choice garments, in clothes of blue and embroidered work, and in carpets of colored stuff, bound with cords and made secure; in these they traded with you. The ships of Tarshish traveled for you with your merchandise.

"So you were filled and heavily laden
in the heart of the seas.

Your rowers have brought you out into the high seas.
The east wind has wrecked you in the heart of the seas.
Your riches, your wares, your merchandise,
   your mariners and your pilots,
your caulkers, your dealers in merchandise,
   and all your men of war who are in you,
with all your company that is in your midst,
sink into the heart of the seas
   on the day of your ruin.
At the sound of the cry of your pilots
   the countryside shakes,
and down from their ships
   come all that handle the oar.
The mariners and all the pilots of the sea
   stand on the shore
and wail aloud over you, and cry bitterly.
They cast dust on their heads and wallow in ashes;
they make themselves bald for you,
   and gird themselves with sackcloth,
and they weep over you in bitterness of soul,
   with bitter mourning.
In their wailing they raise a lamentation for you,
   and lament over you:
'Who was ever destroyed like Tyre in the midst of
   the sea?
When your wares came from the seas
   you satisfied many peoples;
with your abundant wealth and merchandise
   you enriched the kings of the earth.
Now you are wrecked by the seas,
   in the depths of the waters;
your merchandise and all your crew have sunk with you.
All the inhabitants of the coastlands are appalled at you;
and their kings are horribly afraid,
   their faces are convulsed.
The merchants among the peoples hiss at you;

you have come to a dreadful end
and shall be no more forever.' "

The word of the LORD came to me: "Son of man, say to
the prince of Tyre, Thus says the Lord GOD:

"Because your heart is proud,
  and you have said, 'I am a god,
I sit in the seat of the gods,
  in the heart of the seas,'
yet you are but a man, and no god,
  though you consider yourself as wise as a god—
you are indeed wiser than Daniel;
  no secret is hidden from you;
by your wisdom and your understanding
  you have gotten wealth for yourself,
and have gathered gold and silver into your treasures;
by your great wisdom in trade
  you have increased your wealth,
  and your heart has become proud in your wealth—
therefore, behold, I will bring strangers upon you,
  the most terrible of the nations;
and they shall draw their swords
  against the beauty of your wisdom
  and defile your splendor.
They shall thrust you down into the Pit,
  and you shall die the death of the slain
  in the heart of the seas.
Will you still say, 'I am a god,'
  in the presence of those who slay you,
though you are but a man, and no god,
  in the hands of those who wound you?
You shall die the death of the uncircumcised
  by the hand of foreigners;
  for I have spoken, says the Lord GOD."

Moreover the word of the LORD came to me: "Son of man,
raise a lamentation over the king of Tyre, and say to him,
Thus says the Lord GOD:

"You were the signet of perfection, full of wisdom
      and perfect in beauty.
You were in Eden, the garden of God;
every precious stone was your covering,
      carnelian, topaz, and jasper,
      chrysolite, beryl, and onyx,
      sapphire, carbuncle, and emerald;
and wrought in gold were your settings and your
      engravings.
On the day that you were created they were prepared.
With an anointed guardian cherub I placed you;
      you were on the holy mountain of God;
      in the midst of the stones of fire you walked.
You were blameless in your ways
      from the day you were created,
      till iniquity was found in you.
In the abundance of your trade
      you were filled with violence, and you sinned;
so I cast you as a profane thing from the mountain
            of God,
      and the guardian cherub drove you out
      from the midst of the stones of fire.
Your heart was proud because of your beauty;
you corrupted your wisdom for the sake of your splendor.
I cast you to the ground;
I exposed you before kings,
      to feast their eyes on you.
By the multitude of your iniquities,
      in the unrighteousness of your trade
      you profaned your sanctuaries;
so I brought forth fire from the midst of you;
it consumed you,
      and I turned you to ashes upon the earth
      in the sight of all who saw you;
you have come to a dreadful end
      and shall be no more for ever."

                          (Ezek. 27, 28:1-19, RSV)

The tragedy of Tyre was rooted in her narcissistic pride. She fell in love with her greatness and declared herself God. This, in turn, brought on the reaction from all that is creative within God's kingdom. Tyre tumbled, and, like Humpty Dumpty who fell from the wall, all the king's horses and all the king's men could not put her together again. She did not rise from her fall. She was replaced—by the Greeks in the East and her own offspring, the Carthaginians, in the West—until those who took her place were, in turn, replaced by others.

Much nonsense has been written about "the fall of man." It is customary to think that "the fall" is that point at which we step out of the cradle of childhood called the Garden of Eden. But that is not the case. The step out of Eden may lead to a noble "walk with God" as well as the way of Tyre. The biblical fall of man occurs after he has built his kingdom and then attempted to go beyond to make it a kingdom of God. God does not knock us down for the building of kingdoms. He only tumbles us when we build them in honor of false notions of what is God, i.e., when we try to perpetuate our own structures and make them eternal. The judgmental work of the wrath of God is to tumble false kings from their thrones and, thus, declare them the mere mortal men they are.

All this is illustrative of the most basic of all the differences between the kingdoms of God and the kingdoms of men. God's kingdom is eternal. Man's kingdoms are not. Again, it is a prophet of Israel who can state this better than we.

A voice says, "Cry!"
And I said, "What shall I cry?"
All flesh is grass,
and all its beauty is like the flower of the field.
The grass withers, the flower fades,
    when the breath of the LORD blows upon it;
    surely the people is grass.
The grass withers, the flower fades;
but the word of our God will stand for ever.

Behold, the nations are like a drop from a bucket,
and are accounted as the dust on the scales;
behold, he takes up the isles like fine dust.

All the nations are as nothing before him,
accounted by him as less than nothing and emptiness.

It is he who sits above the circle of the earth,
and its inhabitants are like grasshoppers;
who stretches out the heavens like a curtain,
and spreads them like a tent to dwell in;
who brings princes to nought,
and makes the rulers of the earth as nothing.
Scarcely are they planted, scarcely sown,
scarcely has their stem taken root in the earth,
when he blows upon them, and they wither,
and the tempest carries them off like stubble.

(Isa. 40:6-8, 15, 17, 22-24, RSV)

Or the poet who sang,

The Lord thwarts the will of the nations;
he hinders the plan of the peoples,
but his own will endures forever;
the plans of his mind affect ages.

(Ps. 33:10-11, Author)

Human kingdoms exist only by the grace of God. And that same grace sees that they do not exist forever. There is a fitting place for all of them when their days are done. For man, that place is the museums where we honor the greatness of our own past. For God, that place is the grave, which transforms yesterday's life into tomorrow's.

In the twelfth year, in the first month, on the fifteenth day of the month, the word of the LORD came to me: "Son of man, wail over the multitude of Egypt, and send them down, her and the daughters of majestic nations, to the nether world, to those who have gone down to the Pit:

'Whom do you surpass in beauty?

Go down, and be laid with the uncircumcised.'

They shall fall amid those who are slain by the sword, and with her shall lie all her multitudes. The mighty chief shall speak of them, with their helpers, out of the midst of Sheol: 'They have come down, they lie still, the uncircumcised, slain by the sword.'

"Assyria is there, and all her company, their graves round about her, all of them slain, fallen by the sword; whose graves are set in the uttermost parts of the Pit, and her company is round about her grave; all of them slain, fallen by the sword, who spread terror in the land of the living.

"Elam is there, and all her multitude about her grave; all of them slain, fallen by the sword, who went down uncircumcised into the nether world, who spread terror in the land of the living, and they bear their shame with those who go down to the Pit. They have made her a bed among the slain with all her multitude, their graves round about her, all of them uncircumcised, slain by the sword; for terror of them was spread in the land of the living, and they bear

their shame with those who go down to the Pit;
they are placed among the slain.

"Meshech and Tubal are there, and all their multitude, their graves round about them, all of them
uncircumcised, slain by the sword; for they spread
terror in the land of the living. And they do not lie
with the fallen mighty men of old who went down to
Sheol with their weapons of war, whose swords were
laid under their heads, and whose shields are upon
their bones; for the terror of the mighty men was in
the land of the living. So you shall be broken and lie
among the uncircumcised, with those who are slain
by the sword.

"Edom is there, her kings and all her princes, who
for all their might are laid with those who are slain
by the sword; they lie with the uncircumcised, with
those who go down to the Pit

"The princes of the north are there, all of them,
and all the Sidonians, who have gone down in shame
with the slain, for all the terror which they caused
by their might; they lie uncircumcised with those who
are slain by the sword, and bear their shame with
those who go down to the Pit.

"When Pharaoh sees them, he will comfort himself
for all his multitude, Pharaoh and all his army, slain
by the sword, says the Lord GOD. For he spread terror
in the land of the living; therefore he shall be laid
among the uncircumcised, with those who are slain
by the sword, Pharaoh and all his multitude, says the
Lord GOD."

(Ezek. 32:17-32, RSV)

The fundamental thing to assert about the kingdoms
of men is their mortality. Like man himself, they come
from the dust and that is the state to which they must
return. It is entirely fitting that past history is buried
in the soil and can often be retrieved only by the

archeologist's spade. It helps remind us of who we are and of what our kingdoms shall be like when we are gone. It is in the Talmud (Pirke Aboth) that we find this bit of wisdom stated most memorably.

> Akabya ben Mahalalel says: Mark well three things, and thou wilt not fall into the clutches of sin. Know whence thou art come, whither thou art going, and before whom thou art destined to give an account and reckoning.
> "Whence thou art come?"
> From a putrid drop.
> "Wither thou art going?"
> To a place of dust, worm, and maggot.
> "And before whom thou art destined to give an account and reckoning?"
> Before the King of kings, the Holy One, blessed be He.
>
> (As translated in *The Living Talmud* by Judah Goldin, New American Library, p. 118)

There is one kind of human kingdom that is extraordinarily hard to place. It is a kingdom which is essentially religious in character: the synagogue (for Jews) or the church (for Christians). On the one hand, it is clearly of man's building, with all the marks of human creation upon it: structure, organization, rank, human leadership, political intrigue, jealousy between factions, causes for war and strife, the possession of goods and the building of edifices. Certainly, when one looks at these features, the church and the synagogue must be called kingdoms of men and, like kingdoms of men, they should crumble and fall either sooner or later.

And yet these kingdoms stand as symbols for something beyond the trappings that catch our eye. They are signs or tokens of that one kingdom that is eternal. The kingdom called Israel has a dual nature. It is, to be sure, a human affair and can at any moment become purely that in its behavior and, as a consequence, be swallowed by a fish prepared by her master. Yet, like a signet ring or a word, it stands for something beyond itself. It is a sign and a witness, a prophetic testimony to the reality that comprehends us all. That is why life never lets it die. Tyre and Assyria and Babylon fell to rise no more. They were replaced. But the dry bones of Israel were resurrected to live again and declare the glory of him who redeemed them. Jonah is the only man who can survive three days in the belly of a fish. Why? Because God must furnish us all with a witness—lest we perish in the service of the gods we have made.

When the church and synagogue fulfill their holy calling, they make light of their human trappings or even shuck them off and exist as no more than a voice crying in the wilderness. That, after all, is what the world needs. The prophet can do without castle or army or "Inc." after his name. He can even do without supporters and followers if need be. But he cannot do without his voice. He is, after all and before all, the word which preserves us and leads to fulfillment.

Perhaps we have overemphasized the insignificance of human kingdoms. To keep things in proper perspective, let us repeat the biblical injunction to "be fertile and increase, fill the earth and master it, and rule the fish of the sea, the birds of the sky, and all the living things that creep on earth." Within the boundaries of God's encompassing power and of our own native intelligence and common sense, we have been given not only the freedom but the mandate to build. The variety of kingdoms we can build seems to stagger the imagination. In fact, our ability to devise new kinds of worlds only seems to increase. At one time we were satisfied with home and family, farm or shop, and commonly the two were combined. Nowadays, a man may be a citizen of several kingdoms—some large and some small—and they run the gamut from a club that exists for pure pleasure to a government that demands a third of his private means or even his life for the privilege of citizenship.

There is nothing inherently wrong with any of these kingdoms providing we remember: (1) that none of them is forever, (2) that all are within and beneath the kingdom that is God's, (3) that the chief pleasure for men is the building rather than the sustaining of kingdoms and (4) that a human kingdom is most useful and glorious when it is actually put to the service of God's kingdoms.

In regard to the first two points, I would summon the wisdom of *Qoheleth,* who reminds us that none of our creations are quite as original in the eyes of all time as they are to us at the moment of their production, that all human kingdoms are vain ("breathy") things at best and that the real limits of our possibilities can still be described as laboring in the master's vineyard.

> What has been is what will be
> and what has been done is what will be done.

There is nothing new beneath the sun.
Suppose there is something of which they say,
   "See this! It is new."
It has already been in the ages long before us.

There is no remembrance of things from the distant past
and, as for the modern things that take place,
there will be no remembrance of them
   in a still more modern age.

I built myself mansions
and planted me vineyards.
I made myself gardens and parks
and put in them all kinds of fruit trees.
I made myself pools of water
whose moisture could water a forest of growing trees.
I bought slaves, male and female,
who became my household family.
Moreover, I owned more cattle and sheep
   than all who preceded me in Jerusalem.
I even gathered silver and gold
and the treasures of kings and states.
I got myself singers and songstresses
and other kinds of luxuries of men.
I became greater, I increased more,
   than all who preceded me in Jerusalem.
And wisdom remained with me.

I withheld nothing my eyes desired
nor denied my heart any kind of joy,
for my heart found happiness in all my work
and this was my reward for all my labor.

Then I turned to all the deeds that my hands had done
and the work I had had done in doing them.
Behold! It was all futile, a chasing of the wind.
There is nothing profitable beneath the sun.
I turned to look at wisdom:

it was idiocy and foolishness.
What can be done by the man who comes after the king
  who has already done all these things?

Furthermore, I hate all my work at which I have labored
  beneath the sun—the results of which will be left
  to a man who comes after we. Who knows whether
  he will be a wise man or a fool?
  Yet he will become master of all my labors
    —at which *I* labored!
    —at which *I* was so wise beneath the sun!
  This, indeed, is a futile thing.

So I turned around to devote my mind to despair over all
  the works at which I had labored beneath the sun.
  Suppose that a man whose work has been done in
  wisdom and whose energies have been expended in
  knowledge should leave his reward to a man who has
  not labored for it. Is this not, indeed, futile and a
  great evil?
  What becomes of a man for all his work, for the
  striving of his mind in which he labors beneath the sun?
  All his days are painful;
  frustration is his lot.
  Even at night his mind cannot rest.
  This, indeed, is a futile thing.

  It is not good that a man merely eat and drink
  but let him permit his soul to see good in his labor.

  There is nothing better for men than to be happy
  and enjoy themselves as long as they live.
  Yes, that every man should eat and drink
  and see good in his labor,
  this is the gift of God.

Behold what I see to be the good and proper thing: it is to
  eat and drink and see what's good in all the work at
  which you labor beneath the sun every one of the days

of the life which God has given you. This is your
reward. Furthermore, to every man to whom God has
given wealth and treasures and the power to enjoy
them—to accept his reward and find happiness in his
work *is* the gift of God. He does not reminisce much
upon the days of his life, for God keeps him occupied
with happiness in his heart.

The almond tree blossoms,
the grasshopper drags itself along,
the berry drops from its branch.
So man goes to his eternal home
and the mourners walk about in the street.

Before long, the silver chain is severed
and the golden bowl is broken.
The pitcher is in pieces at the fountain
and the wheel lies broken at the pit.
The dust returns to the earth as it was
and the life-spirit returns to God.
                         (Eccles. 1:9-11, 2:4-12 and
                         18-24, 3:12-13, 5:18-20,
                         Author, unpublished)

The lesson is this: if each man can learn to live
within a lifetime and accept his death when it comes
and if each human institution can accept the fact of
its mortal creation and its death as well, the business
of building human kingdoms can be a most delightful
and pleasurable occupation. More important still, if
men can learn to dedicate their private creations and
domains to the service of all God's children, they may
see their seemingly petty kingdoms blest with God's
blessing and giving glory to the King of all kings himself. As surely as a human can be God's servant, so
surely can our kingdoms serve the will of God and
share in the world that is coming.

CHAPTER FOUR

CHANGE AND DECAY

> Remember not the former things,
>   nor consider the things of old
> Behold, I am doing a new thing;
>   now it springs forth, do you not perceive it?
>   (Isa. 43:18-19, RSV)

There is nothing more certain in all the world than the fact that all is changing. "Still life" is a human creation. All that is created by God is in constant movement.

Yet this is difficult for man to accept. "Change and decay in all around I see," a hymn-writer wrote, "O Thou who changest not, abide with me." He struck a chord of yearning that made his hymn an all-time hit. So deep and earnest is our need for something impervious to change that we are apt to deify the first thing we find that seems to be changeless.

In slower times many things appeared changeless: the state, the family name, the church—not to mention such permanent fixtures as the heavenly bodies and earth itself. But, one by one, all these things have either disintegrated before our eyes or been shown to be constantly evolving. Families and states that were supposed to be eternal by divine decree succumbed to death and revolution. The church underwent a fragmentation that cured many of ever having faith in it again. Charles Darwin and his colleagues and predecessors, not to mention every scientist since, showed the world a slow-motion picture of evolution that still seems breathtaking when one first thinks about it. All things are in flux—and perhaps a still more profound truth is this: *if there is anything in all creation that is changeless, it must be sought through those things which change themselves, for nothing but that which changes is accessible to our senses.*

All things in God's greater kingdom are subject to change. Or should we say, all things in God's greater kingdom *are alive with change.* This second way of saying it demands an essentially different perspective and is not only less frightening but more true to reality. If we merely say "subject to change" we are indicating a kind of passivity that is not there, even if we grant that the power doing the changing is God. To picture creation as a passive thing merely subject to the creative power is to think of God as somehow detached from his creation, doing things *with* it and *to* it. The God we meet in the Scriptures is not only "above the circle of the earth." He is, as the writer of Psalm 139 discovered, very much in his world as well. The powers which "cause" change are vital and creative, not manipulatory. Therefore we say "alive with change"—and we think it an exciting insight.

We all (or most of us, at least) accept the phenomenon of change that makes the cycle of a lifetime—the episodes that pass between birth and the grave. We know that we cannot remain children forever, that youth must give way to middle age and that old age will shorten our breath in more than one way. It is often with lingering regret that we move from one stage to another. But despite all nostalgia, nature moves us on. In our wiser moments, we might even see something beautiful in it.

This same cycle of change is apparent in other species. We learn to expect that some of these species have either shorter or longer spans of life than our own. The livestock trader knows very well that a ten-year-old cow is not like a ten-year-old human; none of us expects our cats and dogs to outlive us; and we all thank God for the short life cycle of mosquitoes.

When we think beyond the familiar realm of the life cycles of beasts, men, and plants, however, we discover that it took the studied efforts of philosophers and scientists to show us that this same phenomenon operates all about and within us at great variations of speed. With microscopes and other devices for looking at micro-worlds, we see cycles of life whose rapidity is downright startling and come to know our own bodies as complex factories within which life and death are ever recurring. Then we look out at the heavenly bodies and see gigantic systems exploding into space! Out there and on this planet of ours we become aware of movements so huge that we cannot perceive them except in measured segments. All of the natural phenomena that once were regarded as stable have turned out to be as alive with change as the colors of an evening sunset. We dig into the layers of earth and find fossils of forms that once were and have since been transformed into offspring of only remote resemblance. The moment of life that is ours, in which we view the creation around us, is but one frame in a colossal motion picture that spans millennia of millennia. And the moment we discover this we may well feel like saying "amen" to the rather eloquent closing paragraph of Charles Darwin's famed *Origin of Species.*

> It is interesting to contemplate a tangled bank, clothed with many plants of many kinds, with birds singing on the bushes, with various insects flitting about, and with worms crawling through the damp earth, and to reflect that these elaborately constructed forms, so different from each other, and dependent upon each other in so complex a manner, have all been produced by laws acting around us. These laws, taken in the largest sense, being Growth with reproduction, Inheritance which is almost implied by reproduction, Variability from the indirect and direct action of the conditions of life, and from use and disuse: a Ratio of Increase so high as to lead to a Struggle for Life, and as a consequence improved forms. Thus, from the war of nature, from famine and death, the most exalted object which we are capable of conceiving, namely, the production of the higher animals, directly follows. There is grandeur in this view of life, with its several powers, having been originally breathed by the Creator into a few forms or into one; and that, while this planet has gone circling on according to the fixed law of gravity, from so simple a beginning endless forms most beautiful and most wonderful have been, and are being evolved.

Nor is it as mere spectators that we behold this intricately shifting kaleidoscope. We have our own history as a species and must admit that the process is within as well as around us. We are not today as we were. Perhaps nothing is.

A contemporary scientist states that thought this way:

> We have had a century in which to assimilate the concept of organic evolution, but only recently have we begun to understand that this is only part, perhaps the culminating part, of cosmic evolution. We live in a historical universe, one in which stars and galaxies as well as living creatures are born, mature, grow old, and die. That may indeed be true of the universe as a whole; if so, it appears by some recent estimates to be about 20 billion years old. But whatever doubt is held of the transitory nature of the universe, such a Galaxy as ours surely had a beginning, and pursues its course toward an eventual end; and this, the Milky Way—perhaps 15 billion years old, and about 100,000 light years across, and containing about 100 billion stars—provides a quite adequate stage on which to explore the enterprise of life.

> . . . .

> We living things are a late outgrowth of the metabolism of our Galaxy. The carbon that enters so importantly into our composition was cooked in the past in a dying star. From it at lower temperatures nitrogen and oxygen were formed. These, our indispensable elements, were spewed out into space in the exhalations of red giants and such stellar catastrophes as supernovae, there to be mixed with hydrogen, to form eventually the substance of the sun and planets, and ourselves. The waters of ancient seas set the pattern of ions in our blood. The ancient atmospheres molded our metabolism.

We have been told so often and on such tremendous authority as to seem to put it beyond question, that the essence of things must remain forever hidden from us; that we must stand forever outside nature, like children with their noses pressed against the glass, able to look in, but unable to enter. This concept of our origins encourages another view of the matter. We are not looking into the universe from outside. We are looking at it from inside. Its history is our history; its stuff, our stuff. From that realization we can take some assurance that what we see is real.

(George Wald, "The Origins of Life,"
The Scientific Endeavor, The Rockefeller
Institute Press, pp. 113, 133-34)

The natural world is a veritable showcase with millions of proofs of our axiom: there is nothing more certain in all the world than the fact that all is changing.

Even death in God's greater kingdom is not the end that it seems to be. The bodies that go into the ground as well as those lying on the surface of the soil merely succumb to other forms of life and join the grand cycle in a different shape. The elements are re-used or transformed and the principle of life goes on.

The dust returns to the earth as it was
and the life-spirit goes back to God.
(Eccles. 12:7, Author, unpublished)

You take their breath and they die
and go back to the dust they came from.
Yet you send back the breath and create,
renewing the face of the earth.
(Ps. 104:29-30, Author)

This is an intriguing passage near the end of the Book of Deuteronomy that goes like this.

> So Moses the servant of the Lord died there, in the land of Moab, at the command of the Lord. He buried him in the valley in the land of Moab, near Beth-peor; and no one knows his burial place to this day.

Even more intriguing is a legend found in the Book of Enoch, quoted in the New Testament book of Jude, that the devil contended for the body of Moses. It reveals our human fear about bodies that are not properly buried. Here, again, is our reluctance to accept God's principle of change. In puny defiance we make waterproof, rustproof caskets and embalm our remains to insure some survival beyond death. But the Lord has his way and the elements themselves will have us if the insects and beasts don't get there first.

Moses knew the Lord of Life too well to either run from death or permit a fancy embalmment. Moses walked out to meet him letting God, who envelops us all our lives, enfold him when he died.

Unlike Moses, most people resist change and the possibility of their own deaths, reaching out for the security that they can find in the world. But change itself is eternal. We must do more than accept its inevitability—we must grasp it, clinging to it as though we were its lovers. It will give us the ride of our lives and treat us to thrills beyond belief. Yet only by letting its tides carry us can we know the gracious quality of the powers that move us all.

That may be a frightening way to begin. The message is gospel—good news. Yet, strange as it seems, gospel is often the most frightening thing in all the world to those who are anxious and fearful. The freedom that comes with abandoning oneself to God, looks like death before we let go. It is like pondering a plunge into the ocean. Somehow we think that the certainty of drowning is greater because the waters are wide and deep. Only when we relax and feel for the forces at play do we discover the buoyancy that is there.

What we need is a commitment to the future that is greater than our easy commitments to the past. We must see God, not as the one who used to be—one whose identity is tied only to our patriarchal roots—but as one who beckons us to the future. We must know God as the one who prepares the way for us and invites us to believe in the kingdom that is always coming. Real faith is not based on what we "know for sure." Real faith is commitment to what seems to be the uncertainty of tomorrow. It is trust. This is the faith that Jesus demanded before men could be healed. This, also, is the faith that is described by the anonymous writer of the Epistle to the Hebrews.

> Faith is being sure of the things we hope for, being convinced of the things we can't see.
>
> By faith we know God made the world by His Word so that what we see wasn't made of what can be seen.
>
> Now then, . . . let us get rid of every burden and the sin we easily fall into and with endurance run the

race laid out before us, looking to Jesus, who gives
us our faith from start to finish.

(Heb. 11:1, 3 and 12:1-2, Beck)

The element of change in God's creation will destroy
us only if we resist it. So it is with death. Death in this
kingdom is lost in the larger cycles of life which encompass it. Every death in God's kingdom serves the
birth of a new form of life. Tragedy occurs only when
death brings the world to an end. "He who would find
his life must lose it," said Jesus of Nazareth. He knew
the mystery of which we are speaking if anyone ever
did.

The strangest thing of all (to us) is that the good
as well as the bad must succumb to this judgment of
time. When the Lord of Life "takes hold of the skirts
of the earth and shakes out the wicked" (Job 38:13),
our proudest virtues and accomplishments are in-
cluded. Just as surely as God's creative sun and rain
fail to distinguish between the good and the evil, so
his judgment of death takes the fine with the foul. It
is not just our sins that must give way to his "wrath."
The consuming fire purges all things in preparing for
tomorrow. The floods of time carry all things in their
path to the sea.

You may agree that change is a part of God's kingdom. But what of the kingdoms of men? If there is
any point at which our God-image comes through, it
is here: not only do we like to build kingdoms—we
also like to re-order and re-structure them from time
to time. We sometimes even like change for the sake
of change. To a woman, that may be all that's neces-

sary for a new coat or hat or a reshuffling of the living room furniture. Her husband likes to be more logical about it and bolsters his intuitions with fancy rationale, but, in the final analysis, he may be operating in response to the same basic instinct when he "needs" a new gadget or car. We are double-natured creatures. We want the world about us to be eternally changeless, yet we demand the right to change our own little kingdoms as we please. Why? It is easier to build little kingdoms to suit our fancies if the surrounding environment is not subject to alteration. It is easier if we can regard the world around us as a vast reservoir of resources from which we can draw the materials we need for building and ordering *our* little worlds! If the world about us was no more than a passive pile of lumber, we would never have to conform to it or adjust to the unexpected. We would only have to help ourselves to its abundance when we needed new rooms for our mansions. Not only would this allow us to create our own kingdoms without hindrance, it would also permit us to make up the rules for whatever games we wish to play, without fear that those rules would ever need alteration due to circumstances beyond our control.

But the world around us is not a lumber pile. We can treat it like one, but sooner or later some tornado or similar disaster awakens us to the fact that our environment is a lively place.

Then, of course, we may react with the cleverest of all the things a sick mind can devise. "All right, we may say, "if nothing outside will stand still, I'll make my *own* world eternal." Whereupon we proceed to decide how we shall want things to be forever and labor to make them so. When it suits our fancy, we shall fasten our furniture where we want it to remain and snarl at all who suggest that it might look better another way. The world is full of such eternalized little kingdoms of men and that, most of all, is what makes it such a difficult place for those who know and love freedom.

All of this would be unnecessary if we would satisfy ourselves with the role of being co-builders within God's kingdom—we and all humans together.

It is sad to behold what happens to human kingdoms that refuse to acknowledge the necessity of change. Their healthier citizens become discontent and begin to rebel as the vital forces of their God-given urges and senses ferment within them. Then, as the king on the throne begins to hear the rumblings of their dissatisfaction, he increases his armies of law and order to contain any violence and, with seeming concern and good will on the other hand, doles out whatever he thinks will appease their restlessness. But the best he can do is to postpone the inevitable changes and, in the process, make them all the more radical and violent when they finally arrive.

Change is not a pretty thing when it cannot proceed at its natural and steady pace—when it becomes revolution rather than evolution. If we allow the process of change to happen at its normal pace, it is not particularly frightening. Indeed, it can be vital and exciting. Delayed, however, it turns to violence—as though the pent-up powers of God's world can do nothing but explode in order to break out of their human encasements. Yet even ugly revolutions are striking "proofs" of the "existence" of God. They testify to the fact that the creator will not let creation stop.

Human kingdoms must share this quality of change that is the very essence of all God's worlds. If they do not, they must expect to face violent upheaval and destruction. When a human kingdom stops changing, one can be sure that its leadership is senile and death is not far away. *The final word we can speak about change is this: if we will not permit it to do its life-giving work, it will grind out the death of all that matters most dearly to us, for change and decay are the mighty will of the living God.*

CHAPTER FIVE

WARS AND RUMORS OF WARS

There are fundamentally two kinds of conflict in this world: the conflicts between the kingdoms of men and the conflict that arises when human kingdoms defy the kingdom of God.

To speak of the first would seem to be a simple matter. It accounts for much of the "stuff of life" we see around us every day and ranges in degree from mild "conflict of interests" to open warfare and, in scope, from a toy-throwing battle in a sandbox to the world wars that have characterized our century. In its grandest scale it always seems too complicated to understand (usually because there are more than two kingdoms in conflict), so let us look for its essential ingredients in the minor episodes that involve us from day to day. For example, a family fight between a sister and a brother.

"You've got my chair," says he.

"No I don't, you dummy!" retorts his sister. "The chair was sittin' here empty when I came along and, besides, it couldn't be yours anyway 'cuz it belongs to the whole family."

"But I had it first," argues her brother. "I was usin' it to watch TV and then I had to go make my bed because Ma told me to and you took it when I was gone."

"So? If you'd made your bed like you were s'posed to, you could've kept your old chair. It's mine now, 'cus *I'm* usin' it."

Now we can well imagine that brother will appeal to parental authority somewhere along in the argument, that the fight will extend to other areas of conflict and that older matters of contention will be brought in, that there will be a mutual declaration of rights and an assertion something like the following:

"All right. *Keep* your old chair! See if I care. But don't you dare set foot in my *room* or don't you ever try to use any of my *toys* any more. You're always taking things that belong to me—like you own the whole world or something."

All of this is in the interest of establishing and maintaining a dominion that each can call his own and rule with some degree of autonomy and freedom. We rise in defense when we feel that our kingdoms are threatened; we are moved to attack and make conquests if we think our domains are too small.

All would go well if there were no limits of space and resources. But other kinglets and queenlets have interests like ours, putting a strain on both space and resources. Indeed, we may have to turn to the conquest of people and the establishment of gangs for the sake of fulfilling this desire when space and objects are lacking. Increase of human population complicates this mad race immensely.

The size of the kingdom each person demands seems to vary in accord with at least two other factors: potential and security.

Some people seem to be born with a greater capacity for dominion than others. They hardly leave the cradle before we see a little general on the march or tomorrow's governor getting ready for his office. And the rest of us don't resent this much as long as the president-to-be operates within the limits of his capabilities and with respect for the welfare of others. We expect some folks to be leaders and allow them to exercise their role.

Security is another matter. It would seem that a person who is given the proper love and protection as a child is most apt to be satisfied with his natural limitations when he matures. A person who is starved of affection and security may become a dangerous man—a vicious marauder or a paranoid crank.

People who feel secure are not warmakers. Peace is much more to their interests and so they resolve their conflicts with others before they reach dangerous proportions. A man starved of love, on the other hand, may never get enough. He may enter a cycle of insecurity and aggression that will lead to ridiculous behavior. His initial insecurity may drive him to possess more than he can manage and his inability to manage his over-extended domain may lead to even greater fear of loss. The more fearful he becomes, the more he must possess. The more he possesses, the more he fears the loss of what he has. He will have to erect elaborate defenses to protect his holdings and put severe restrictions on whom he can trust in his castle. In the end he will be a lonesome king in a colossal fort, exterminating, hedging in, or buying off every potential foe.

The antics of nations are no less comic than the power games played by individual people when one can view them from any distant perspective. In spite of all noble rationale, the percentages of national incomes that must go for "defense" betray our degree of fear and mistrust. Our knowledge of our own desires to gobble up what is around us makes us highly suspicious of our neighbors. If another nation shows any spirit of competition, we are quick to shore up our defenses and stockpile armaments. There is no such thing as voluntary deescalation without a surrender of national pride and an acknowledgment that one's day of glory is declining. As long as a nation is building its power and glory, it will demand an increase of its military might to match every threat it can imagine.

In view of these facts, the only practical morality to be followed in international politics is to resolve all conflicts while they are still small, especially since the escalation of arms will insure our mutual destruction if ever the giants of national power engage in a full-scale war. Our present capabilities of destruction make it absolutely essential that we cultivate and develop every device short of war that we know for the resolution of international conflicts. The world cannot tolerate armed conflict between the giants of our day because the weapons we have at our disposal threaten the safety and welfare of too many lives.

But what, besides war, can resolve our conflicts? The conference table usually turns out to be a game of masks in which the very confrontation that is needed for the resolution of conflict is gingerly avoided. It is still far superior to the battlefield, however, and ought to become a place of regular meeting in the hope that we will, with practice, learn how to resolve issues with words.

The delegation of power to a world authority seems premature. The problem is simple: any nation that has a good deal of power and security is not about to relinquish much of it for the sake of something which will surely outrank it. Only the little countries want a powerful United Nations, for they have so little to lose in might and so much to gain in protection.

The games that have been played since the founding of the UN have been tragically funny. With characteristic bluntness, the Communist bloc has refused to take it seriously enough to let it function in cases where it is involved. The leaders of "the West" act with equally characteristic self-deception, putting the UN into action when it suits the cause of our kind of justice but conveniently side-stepping and circumventing it when it cannot support our version of "freedom" and guarantee our particular interest. The insane things that go on between Israel and the UN Security Council are only a parody of the same behavior between the United States and the United Nations.

Certainly the thing that is most needed is a weaken-

ing of ideologies and a freeing of the human minds
that attempt to guide the destinies of nations. We are
safe only when leaders will act on the basis of reason
rather than fear. But what are the chances of having
reasonable men in positions of power? Where power
is self-perpetuating the chances would seem to be slim.
But are they much better in a democratic system?
When the citizens of a nation are afraid, they will
elect a man who feels their fears and responds to them.
Paranoid people are apt to elect a paranoid leader.
The world should never forget that Adolf Hitler was
first elected in a popular election—simply because he
catered to the injured pride and insecurity of the Ger-
man people.

Enough of this commentary on the conflicts between
human kingdoms. We turn to conflicts between our
kingdoms and the kingdom of God and find them
sufficiently complicated to demand a detailed discussion of many points.

We must begin with the problem of definition:
many kingdoms of men insist upon taking *themselves*
to be the kingdom of God, regarding all their wars as
the holy wars of God against the infidels. There are,
then, many claims to the title *kingdom of God*. If we
cannot see through them to what legitimately deserves
that title, we shall mistake human conflicts of interest
for the struggle between God and men. All sorts of
human kingdoms have wanted to be sanctioned as
divine. The Roman Empire felt a compulsion to call
itself *Holy,* the European colonial powers spoke of
their conquests as "for the Cross," and there is every
sign that at least one generation of Americans sees

itself as a world Messiah. The myth of the United States of America as "the leader of the free world" seems to fit with this concept, allowing us to identify all our warring "against the Communists" with the cause of God himself—the salvation for which all men should be thankful.

We must repeat here that no human-governed regime is the kingdom of God. The kingdom of God consists of those things which God has created and continues to create. Governments are human creations despite all divine decrees permitting us to create them and, therefore, kingdoms of men. They are not necessarily evil. The very process of kingdom building is a response to the nature life gave us. But we must not *confuse* the two kinds of kingdoms, lest we try to make something eternal of that which is not, or defy our Creator in the very process of fighting for what we *think* is his.

Not even the churches can qualify as kingdoms of God. Even though their concerns remain fundamentally those of God's realm, the most we can call any such reality is a *symbol* of God's kingdom.

It seems quite apparent that any movement which calls itself the church cannot be what it is apart from institutional organization and the possession of at least some of the features of human government. The moment it takes on these characteristics it becomes a human kingdom. Indeed, it runs all the risks of any human kingdom and may well exhibit every kind of vice to which such kingdoms fall victim. The history of the Christian church bears more than eloquent testimony to that observation.

The story of the pre-Exilic era of Israel is a striking example of what we mean. Here was a kingdom that could call itself God's on the grounds that it had been called into existence by his ultimate power. Its poets could speak of Mount Zion as the dwelling place of the Lord and call its temple his sanctuary. They could refer to the kings of the line of David as the anointed sons of Yahweh. No prophetic voice rebuked them for speaking that way. But when they went to the extreme of thinking that their identity as God's people excluded others from his lordship or exempted them from the trials of history, they were roundly rebuked. A quotation from Jeremiah is an example of the indictment.

> Do not put your trust in that lie: "This is Yahweh's temple, Yahweh's temple, Yahweh's temple!" No! Only if you really reform your whole pattern of conduct—if you really behave justly one toward another, no longer oppress the alien, the orphan, and the widow [nor shed innocent blood in this place], nor follow other gods to your own hurt—only then can I dwell with you in this place, in the land that I gave to your fathers of old for all time to come.
>
> Look! You are putting your trust in a worthless lie! What? You think you can steal, murder, commit adultery, perjure yourselves, burn sacrifices to Baal, and follow other gods of whom you know nothing, and then come and stand before me in this house, which bears my name, and say, "We are safe!"—just so you can go right on doing all these abominations? A robber's hideout—is that what this house, which bears my name, has become in your opinion? But look! I too can see—Yahweh's word. Yes, go, if you will, to my place that used to be in Shiloh, where I

first established my residence, and see what I did to
it because of the wickedness of my people Israel. And
now, because you have done all these things—Yahweh's word—and did not listen, though I spoke to
you earnestly and persistently, nor answer when I
called you, I will treat the house which now bears
my name, and in which you place your trust, the
place which I provided for you and your fathers
before you, just as I treated Shiloh. And I will cast
you out of my sight, just as I cast out all those kins-
men of yours, Ephraim's entire progeny.

(Jer. 7:4-15, ANB)

Israel's national identity was not the same as God's,
even though she derived all that identity from God's
calling and his gifts. The most precious symbols of
her identity could be sacrificed in the interest of something far more important. It would seem, in fact, that
Israel's fulfillment of her priestly role was possible
without all the features common to national identity.
She could be the people of God though ruled by
Persians, Greeks, or Romans. Such is the thrust of the
prophecies in the latter half of the Book of Isaiah and
in the parable of Jonah.

Perhaps the greatest of Israel's prophets was the one
who saw her end as a nation and the beginning of a
new kind of Israel which should never need a national
identity for survival or the fulfillment of its mission.

As he was going out of the temple, one of his
disciples said to him, "Teacher, look at those wonder-
ful stones and buildings!" "You see these large
buildings?" Jesus asked him. "Not a stone will be left
on another here but will be torn down."

(Mark 13:1-2, Beck)

Perhaps the most significant thing about the New Testament is that it proclaims a new people of God in which there is neither Jew nor Greek. Not that this new Israel is any more the kingdom of God than the old. It is only a new *kind* of witness to God's domain. That, after all, is the task of Israel: to "bear witness," to "proclaim the glory" of the Creator who calls her, to announce the reality and the coming of God's kingdom.

Many Jewish scholars and Christian theologians have wrestled over the role of the "people of God." But does not this concept of witness-bearer resolve it all? It prevents us from assuming special status or exemptions—or waging wars to extend "God's kingdom"—yet ties us to the task that necessitates our existence.

The real kingdom of God is not a thing that can be either possessed or controlled by men. It is something that comprehends us all and puts special demands on those who listen and see. It is the reality that moves us to the future. And because it moves us—exerts pressure and authority and will—it counters our own claims to power. Because God is God and insists on being so and because men cannot quite buy that demand, we often see conflict between the kingdoms of men and the kingdom of God. This is the struggle between "flesh" and "spirit" that is spoken of in the New Testament. It is also what John means when he speaks of the hatred that "the world" has for the witnesses of God's kingdom and the presence of "the Light."

Such conflict occurs when any kingdom of man is made to be more than it is, asserting itself as some kind of kingdom of God—a phenomenon that occurs so frequently that a good third of what the Old Testament prophets had to say was on this very point. We quote two examples.

And now for Assyria, the whip of my anger
And the lash of my indignation!
I send him against a faithless nation,
I command him to attack the people who have
     angered me,
To rob them of their treasure and seize their wealth,
To trample them down like mud in the streets.
But this is not how he thinks,
And this is not his plan.
His intention is to destroy;
To exterminate many nations.
He says, Are not my captains as good as kings?
What difference is there between Calno and Carchemish,
Between Hamath and Arpad?
What difference is there between Samaria and Damascus?
Since my own hand has seized idol-loving kingdoms,
Whose graven images were bigger that those
     of Jerusalem and Samaria,
Shall I not treat Jerusalem and her idols
     as I have treated Samaria and her images?

When the Lord has completed his work on mount Zion and on Jerusalem, he will punish the impudent boasting of the king of Assyria for his arrogant pride, for he says:

By the strength of my own hand have I done this,
And by my clever plans—for I am a man
     of understanding.
I have moved the frontiers of nations,
I have robbed them of their treasures;
I have toppled their kings into the dust!
My hand has reached out, as if into a nest,

To grasp the wealth of the nations.
Like a man collecting eggs
I have ransacked the whole earth;
And no one fluttered a wing at me,
And none dared open his beak in protest!

Is the axe to set itself up against him who wields it?
Is the saw to think itself greater than he who uses it?
It would be like a stick swinging the man who lifts it,
Or a wooden staff brandishing a man,
    who is no thing of wood!
Therefore the Lord, the Lord of hosts,
Shall send a wasting sickness into his flourishing body,
Beneath his glory a fire will be kindled
Which burns like a flame,
Consuming soul and body,
Till he wastes away like a man diseased.

(Isa. 10:5-18, Phillips)

Then it shall be that when the Lord has given you rest from
your toil and misery, from the hard labor which you had to
endure, then you will sing a song of contempt to the king
of Babylon, and you will say:

How has the Tyrant fallen,
And the Terror ceased to be!
The Lord has broken the staff of the wicked
And the sceptre of those who ruled,
Which struck the peoples in fury
With never-ending blows;
Which trod down the nations in anger,
In unrelenting wrath.
Now the whole earth lies quietly at peace,
And a song is on every lip.
The very cypresses are joyful,
The cedars of Lebanon cry aloud,
Since you were laid low,
None comes now to cut us down!

The underworld is all agog
To meet you when you come,
Summoning up ghosts for you—
Those who were leaders on earth;
Raising from their thrones
The kings of the nations
To greet you, one and all,
And say, So you too are as weak as we are,
You have become like one of us!
Your glory is brought down to the underworld
With all your sounds of music.
A mattress of maggots lies ready
With a blanket of worms to cover you.

How you have fallen from heaven on high,
You shining son of the dawn!
How you are cut down to the ground,
You who laid all nations low!
You who once said in your heart,
I will scale the skies;
I will set up my throne on high
Above the stars of God,
That I may rule on the mount of the gods,
In the far high places of the North.
I will climb above the towering clouds
And be like God Most High!
Yet down to the underworld shall you be brought
To the dark, deep places of the Pit!

The onlookers stare hard at you
Considering you with narrowed eyes—
Is this the man who caused the earth to tremble
And its kingdoms to quake in fear,
Who turned the world into a wilderness
And its cities into heaps of rubble,
Who never set a prisoner free
To go back to his home?
The kings of the nations sleep in glory,

Each in his own tomb;
But you are thrown out without a grave,
Like a hated monstrous birth,
Flung down among the corpses
Of the men who were slain by the sword.

Those who go down to the depths of the Pit,
A carcase under men's feet.
You shall not join your fathers in the grave!
For you have ruined your country,
And destroyed your own people.
May the names of this evil man's sons
Never be heard upon earth!
Prepare his sons for slaughter,
To die for their father's guilt,
Lest they rise up and possess the earth,
And cover the world with their cities.
(Isa. 14:3-21, Phillips)

The typical sin of the great nations of old, according to Israel's prophets, was this vain pride in which they foolishly asserted themselves as gods. Whenever they made such assertions it was *in the name of a god*— Assur for Assyria, Marduk for Babylon, a dozen divine manifestations for Egypt. Their deities were nothing more than the spirits of the empires themselves. By setting up the pride of their states as gods they were challenging the real power of history with a lie. That challenge called forth the response of God's kingdom: the God-given yearning for freedom in the breast of every man subject to their powers found the same urge in the breast of another, and together they rose up in unity to oppose the oppressor.

It is the better part of human nature which provides

the positive force for breaking human kingdoms that stand in defiance of God. The negative factor assisting this destruction is the same weakness that gnaws from within as the human kingdom over-extends itself. This was strikingly seen in the downfall of Hitler's regime. The loss of the will to fight was as significant as the might of the allied armies in the final moments of the war.

This is significant. God operates through the "human nature" of the people he created in bringing about the fall of human kingdoms. This is the secret of the judging power of God in history. Contrary to a popular misconception, God is not an arbitrary judge in the heavens playing war games—deciding when one nation shall be conquered by another or when a battle shall be lost or won. Such a caricature pays tribute to something other than the biblical God. The God whom we meet in the scriptures is that very power that we "see" in the natural world of which we are part. It is precisely the working of his "natural laws" that brings about judgment. It is when kingdoms made by men violate the rights and needs of God's human beings that judgment can be predicted. Conflict occurs between the kingdoms of men and the kingdom of God when the kingdoms we build suppress the nature of our being, when people are made to exist for the sake of governmental authority, and governments become masters rather than servants, when the kingdoms we build become such mighty ends in themselves that they dehumanize us in our efforts to sustain them. When men must deny their basic needs and live and die only for the sake of extending the life of a crumbling kingdom, they have defied the very grace of God within them.

We are saying that the principles at work in the world of God's creation inexorably grind away and keep all human kingdoms within limits. When any human kingdom defies those laws it is surely doomed for destruction. Its citizens, even its rulers, may very well survive as human beings, but not as proud members of that kingdom. Indeed, the whole purpose of the judging process is to keep men human—to exalt those who are forced into serfdom and slavery and bring down those who are haughty. This is the work of God in history: to tear imperial powers from their thrones and lift the humble, to satisfy the hungry, and send the rich away empty. Many passages of the Bible testify to this activity of God. We choose from the many, two powerful psalms.

> God has stood up in his council,
> passing judgment among the gods.
> > Why do you judge unjustly?
> > Why let the wicked go free?
> > Justify the weak, the fatherless!
> > Vindicate the poor, the afflicted!
> > Rescue the weak, the needy!
> > Deliver from the hand of the wicked!

> They know not; they understand nothing.
> They walk in the dark
> while Earth's foundations are trembling.

> > It was I who said you are gods—
> > every one of you—sons of The Highest.
> > But now, like men, you shall die;
> > like any other prince you shall fall.

Arise, O God, and govern the earth,
for you now inherit all nations!

(Ps. 82, Author)

Praise The Lord!
Give praise, O servants of The Lord!
Give praise to the name of The Lord!
Let the name of The Lord be blest now and forever!

From the rising of the sun to its setting,
let the name of The Lord be praised!
The Lord is above all the nations;
his glory exceeds the heavens.
Who compares to The Lord, our God
  —seated so high
    that he bends to look down
    on both Heaven and Earth?

Yet he raises the poor from the dust;
he lifts the weak from the asphalt
to give them a seat beside princes,
  with the noblest of his people.
He brings barren women back home,
rejoicing because they have sons.
Praise The Lord!

(Ps. 113, Author)

The Old Testament prophets saw this encounter between the divine and the human with extraordinary clarity and it led them to denounce many human regimes. It led them to denounce any efforts on the part of Israel to become too much like those kingdoms or to rely on their promises or support for the sake of her national security. Though she was but a human kingdom herself, the distinctiveness of her role demanded that she live for the sake of God's kingdom, heeding its powers and concerns. When and if she should fail to do this, the justification for her existence would be gone. She would be no more "God's people" in the vocational sense, but would join those who are ignorant of their sonship.

I once came across a fabulous children's tale that could illustrate our point quite well. It was in bouncy poetic form and it was about a turtle who felt that he was too big for the pond in which he lived. He thirsted for kingdom and power and, to satisfy the needs that he felt, he called on some of his fellow turtles to give him a boost that would lift him beyond the horizons of the peaceful little pond in which they all enjoyed the pleasures of life together.

Without questioning his demand, nine of his brethren obeyed and, climbing one upon another, manufactured a living throne for his service. He ascended and discovered a world beyond his pond that amazed him. There, in a world that had been screened from his view by a fringe of green bank growth, were forms he had never imagined: bushes and cats and houses and cows and all such things not native to a water hole.

But what amazed him only made him thirst for more. So he called for more turtles and, at his behest, they stacked themselves up to a tower of impressive dimension—from which he discovered still more strange sights. Confusing what he saw with what he could control, the heroic turtle declared himself ruler of the whole panorama.

At this point, the turtle at the bottom of the turtle-stack began to complain of the load—only to be sharply censured by the self-appointed king of them all who silenced him with the observation that no plain, ordinary turtle has the right to challenge one who is far above him. Then, as if to prove his greatness in one grand gesture of power, his majesty assayed to increase the horizons of his kingdom by calling for still more turtles to pile themselves up beneath him.

The turtles who were still freely swimming in the pond below were so awed by his sudden prestige that they came scrambling to serve him and, like so many who have difficulty questioning authority, valiantly fulfilled his ridiculous wish. The result was colossal: a tower of turtles that reached to the clouds!

Having exhausted his immediate resources, the top turtle seemed momentarily satisfied and began to boast of his greatness—proclaiming himself absolute ruler over all that his gaze could comprehend. But then came a blow that shook him to the core of his ego. As evening darkened, the moon appeared on the horizon and began to climb serenely in the sky. The heroic king gasped. What was this thing that dared to challenge his position of preeminence? What was this that dared to rise higher than he? In frantic rage he began to call for more turtles that he might outclimb the ascending moon.

But at just that moment a natural catastrophe intervened. The bottom turtle, cracking under the strain, lost all control and . . . . well, he burped. And that one little burp caused a tremor in the stack that sent the great king on a dizzying plunge into the humble pond out of which he had risen to his awesome position of power. Of mud he was made; to the mud he returned.

And that's how the tale ended—with the vain-glorious turtle properly subjected and he and the world around him in their proper place. That which stands above all creaturely kingdoms—yet gives to each the simple gift of life and being from within—had prevailed. Life likes us best when we observe our limitations and history tolerates our productions only when they don't have to be eternal.

"Now is this world judged," says Jesus in John 12:31, and the judgment declares that it be no more than what it is, that it be divested of all vain presumptions and deprived of its false gods and the prince of darkness who personifies them all, that it admit the lordship of him who is truly God and listen to whomever he sends to declare that lordship. The judgment is kind, even though it destroy every work of our hands, for through it we discover the glory of what we really are: children of God. This is the saving of the world for which the Messiah appeared. This is the revelation of life that is eternal because it opposes and overcomes the kingdoms that are destined for death.

There is a difficult section near the close of each of the synoptic gospels in the New Testament. It is the scene in which Jesus designates "wars and rumors of wars" as signs of the coming of God's kingdom. How can this be? That the healing of the sick and forgiving of sins should be such signs seems plausible. But that "kingdom rising against kingdom," along with "earthquakes" and "famine" should be signs—what sense lies there?

The sense is this: as human kingdoms rise against each other they betray themselves for what they are and we are no longer so tempted to let them be gods in our eyes. Our loyalties are released to worship God, and we give ourselves to those interests that supersede the kingdoms of men. Moreover, as the powers of God's realm (earthquakes and other such catastrophes of nature) wreak their "vengeance," we are drawn to recognize forces which make our mightiest creations look small. We are moved to fear only what we really need to fear, like the sensible men of today who have far more respect for the power of the atom than the potentials of presidents.

Conflict can show us the true God. As the weak pretenders topple and fall, they disqualify themselves. The forces of God's making emerge as those things which must really be reckoned with, and God reigns supreme—King of all kings and Lord of all lords, now and forever, as it was in the beginning.

CHAPTER SIX

EVEN SO, COME

The aim of this final chapter is to teach us to pray the prayer with which the early Christians culminated the Supper of the Lord, "even so, come, Lord Jesus."

We asserted the reality of one greater kingdom of God to which all men and creatures belong. The implications of this are clear: we should love the Lord above all things and love our neighbor as ourselves. This demands that all other loyalties bow before our loyalty to God—that all other facts of life give precedence to the fact that all men are brothers. But, it must go beyond that. To assert the truth of One God is to allow no special God for humans. Like St. Francis, we must see our kinship with the rest of God's creatures. If we believe in the oneness of God, we must be one with all creation and find our identity within that framework. One scientist (a modern sort of Francis) has worded this beautifully.

> I am a man who has spent a great deal of his life on his knees, though not in prayer. I do not say this

last pridefully, but with the feeling that the posture, if not the thought behind it, may have had some final salutary effect. I am a naturalist and a fossil hunter, and I have crawled most of the way through life. I have crawled downward into holes without a bottom, and upward, wedged into crevices where the wind and the birds scream at you until the sound of a falling pebble is enough to make the sick heart lurch. In man, I know now, there is no such thing as wisdom. I have learned this with my face against the ground. It is a very difficult thing for a man to grasp today, because of his power; yet in his brain there is really only a sort of universal marsh, spotted at intervals by quaking green islands representing the elusive stability of modern science—islands frequently gone as soon as glimpsed.

It is our custom to deny this; we are men of precision, measurement and logic; we abhor the unexplainable and reject it. This, too, is a green island. We wish our lives to be one continuous growth in knowledge; indeed, we expect them to be. Yet well over a hundred years ago Kierkegaard observed that maturity consists in the discovery that "there comes a critical moment where everything is reversed, after which the point becomes to understand more and more that there is something which cannot be understood."

When I separated the serpent from the bird and released them in that wild upland [reference to an experience of freeing a bird from a serpent's grasp], it was not for knowledge; not for anything I had learned in science. Instead, I contained, to put it simply, the serpent and the bird. I would always contain them. I was no longer one of the contending vapors; I had embraced them in my own substance and, in some insubstantial way, reconciled them, as I had sought reconciliation with the muskrat on the shore.

I had transcended feather and scale and gone beyond them into another sphere of reality. I was trying to give birth to a different self whose only expression lies again in the deeply religious words of Pascal, "You would not seek me had you not found me."

I had not known what I sought, but I was aware at last that something had found me. I no longer believed that nature was either natural or unnatural, only that nature now appears natural to man. But the nature that appears natural to man is another version of the muskrat's world under the boat dock, or the elusive sparks over which the physicist made his trembling passage.

(Loren Eiseley in *The Firmament of Time,* pp. 176-78)

If there is but one God, we must allow nothing else to take that important place. Family allegiance, national pride, duty to "one's own"—all must give way to what we owe this One from whom we have derived all things. If there is but one kingdom to which we all belong, then all our divisions of "race," "nationality" or even "creed" must have little meaning to us. "There is one thing that binds us closer than our common faith," said my home town pastor one Sunday. "It is the fact that we all are human." I wished he could have said it in every pulpit of the land.

The concept of one great kingdom of God demands that we join the cause of the new breed of scientists who are excited about a thing called *ecology.* It means that we must stop polluting our rivers and air, acting as though we were strangers here. It means that we see ourselves as part of the grand world that we are fortunate enough to live in. We must blend our praise of the Creator with the warbled song of every bird, the hum and click of every insect, and all the sub- and super-sonic sounds that all the movement about us can produce.

Not that this will disengage us from the world of men about us. We can be as active as anyone, but our perspective will be unique. We will have a sense of humor about all this activity of man and, precisely because we have a sense of humor about it, we may be able to enjoy it more than those who engage themselves with such earnestness that it is a matter of life and death.

For those of us who feel called to be Israel there is a special imperative. It is to get out of our parking lots and start proclaiming the glory of God as though our very existence depended on it. For it does. Unless we testify to God and his world in all that we say and do, our existence as the kingdom of prophets and priests is called into question and we are as useless as broken tools. Our time, like every time, is a moment that will be lost forever. If we do not sound forth the message to this generation, this generation will never hear it. Salvation of all that is proper and joyful. Salvation of praise. Salvation of virtue. Salvation of every good thing that is supposed to be happening to us.

"Whom shall we send?" said the Lord. Dare we say, "Here we are. Send us"? Dare we take up the job when we hear the next word—the warning that it shall be a thankless task?

> "Go, and say to this people:
> Hear and hear, but do not understand;
> see and see, but do not perceive.
> Make the heart of this people fat,

and their ears heavy,
and shut their eyes;
lest they see with their eyes,
and hear with their ears,
and understand with their hearts,
and turn and be healed,"

Then I said, "How long, O Lord?" And he said:

"Until cities lie waste without inhabitant,
and houses without men,
and the land is utterly desolate,
and the Lord removes men far away,
and the forsaken places are many
in the midst of the land.
And though a tenth remain in it,
it will be burned again,
like a terebinth or an oak,
whose stump remains standing when it is felled."

The holy seed is its stump.

(Isa. 6:9-14, RSV)

As for you—gird up your loins!
Stand up and say to them whatever I tell you to say.
Don't lose your nerve because of them,
Lest I shatter your nerve right before them.
And I—see! I have made you today
A fortified city, an iron pillar,
A wall of bronze against all the land:
Against Judah's kings and princes,
Its priests and landed gentry.
Attack you they will; overcome you they can't,
For I'm with you to come to your rescue.

(Jer. 1:17-18, ANB)

The world about us may not listen, but life requires
of the watchman only that he do the watchman's task.

We can do no more than sound the cry. But we can at least do that.

The most exciting imperative of all is the one demanded by the recognition of the third sense in which we can use the phrase *Kingdom of God:* the reality of the future. We brought a scientist-theologian into our first discussion of this topic, in chapter two. Here we quote the words of one who claims to be only a scientist, a man we quoted earlier in this chapter, Loren Eiseley.

> Man is not totally compounded of the nature we profess to understand. Man is always partly of the future, and the future he possesses a power to shape. "Natural" is a magician's word—and like all such entities, it should be used sparingly lest there arise from it, as now, some unglimpsed, unintended world, some monstrous caricature called into being by the indiscreet articulation of worn syllables. Perhaps, if we are wise, we will prefer to stand like those forgotten humble creatures who poured little gifts of flints into a grave. Perhaps there may come to us then, in some such moment, a ghostly sense that an invisible doorway has been opened—a doorway which, widening out, will take man beyond the nature that he knows.
>
> (pp. 180-81)

Does man have the power to shape the future? If he is part of that future, if the future is more within him than in any other species (in terms of the thoughts of his mind at least), he must also have something to do with its happening. As a theologian I would be much more inclined to say that the future is in God's hands. Having said that, however, I would have to go on to say that it is with man—or *in* man and *through* man—that the Lord of life is shaping that future and, therefore, it is very surely man who is involved in the shaping. In submitting to that involvement we shall "go beyond the nature that we know."

If we allow the thoughts of such a one as Teilhard de Chardin to lead us, we must view ourselves as a (or the) segment of creation that is most in evolution at this point, moving toward a consummation of glory that the most daring among us can scarcely imagine. We are the ones who bear the possibility of being born anew—"from above" (an equally valid meaning of the term *anothen*). When we sing "finish then, thy new creation" we are praying a prayer that can do revolutionary things to *ourselves.*

When Jesus of Nazareth spoke of "the kingdom of God" (or "Heaven" in Matthew), he spoke about a reality that has yet to be realized or is only in process of coming into being. What his eyes saw was not apparent to most of his contemporaries because it was still hidden. Its justice was a strange justice and the way it beckoned men still strikes us as amazing for its impossibilities. He saw the vision of the world that not only could be but would be as the will of God pursued its course.

Yet he was not the first to see such a vision. Can anyone see beyond the vision of Isaiah 2:2-4 (Micah 4:1-4)?

> In the last days it will come to pass
> That the mountain of the Lord
> Shall tower above the peaks,
> Lifted high above the hills,
> And all the nations shall swarm to it!

Many peoples will arrive and say,
Come, let us go up to the mountain of the Lord,
And to the house of the God of Jacob.
He will give us knowledge of his ways,
And we will follow in his paths.
For the Law goes forth from Zion,
And the Word of the Lord from Jerusalem.
And he will judge between the nations,
And make decision between the peoples.
Then they shall hammer their swords into ploughshares
And their spears into pruning hooks.
Nation shall lift no sword against nation
And never again will they learn to make war.

(Phillips)

This is not mere optimism. It is the perception of something that most of us do not have the eyes to see. To be sure, some of those who see that new world (though surely not Jesus or Isaiah or Micah) fail to see the enormity of the forces that hold it back, but that does not invalidate the vision they see. It is real and it is the reality that is coming upon us.

The process by which it comes is described by John as *God overcoming the world*. In the Book of Revelation the event is described as *the kingdom of this world becoming the kingdom of our Lord and of his Christ* (11:15).

The reality that is seen is God being God. Not just in fact but in the perception of humanity as well. That is the point of it all: that man shall ultimately *know* God and, in knowing God, truly know himself. It is not enough that man should be a creature. It is destined that he shall also be a son in the household of God and fully cognizant of that. It is not enough that

God should sit on Mount Zion. It is destined that people shall flow to that mountain. The fact that God is
God cannot be changed. What needs to be changed
and is being changed is man's inability to see.

The Adam into whose nostrils Yahweh breathed
the breath of life was not the finished product. Nor is
the neurotic lot of *individuals* we see today. At this
point in time we see adolescents—a people more concerned with the threats to their identity than anything
else and far too insecure and introspective to act like
adults. In our completion we shall be as much one
humanity as God is One God. "It does not yet appear
what we shall be," said John. And yet enough appeared before his eyes that he was able to name it the
koinonia (fellowship) and touch with his hands what
was bringing it into being.

Paul's writings on this point are difficult to understand. But let us look at what he says and see where
it takes us. "Remember that you were once separated
from Christ," he says in his letter to the Ephesians,

> alienated from the commonwealth of Israel, and
> strangers to the covenants of promise, having no hope
> and without God in the world. But now in Christ
> Jesus you who once were far off have been brought
> near in the blood of Christ. For he is our peace, who
> has made us both one, and has broken down the
> dividing wall of hostility, by abolishing in his flesh
> the law of commandments and ordinances, and that
> he might create in himself one new man in place of
> the two, so making peace, and might reconcile us
> both to God in one body through the cross, thereby
> bringing the hostility to an end. And he came and
> preached peace to you who were far off and peace to

those who were near; for through him we both have
access in one Spirit to the Father. So then you are
no longer strangers and sojourners, but you are fellow
citizens with the saints and members of the household
of God, built upon the foundation of the apostles and
prophets, Christ Jesus himself being the cornerstone,
in whom the whole structure is joined together and
grows into a holy temple in the Lord; in whom you
also are built into it for a dwelling place of God in
the spirit.

(Eph. 2:12-22, RSV)

Paul is not just trying to magnify Jesus. He is seeing
in the messianic role all that the claim implies, the
future beginning to happen. When God asserts his
rule over us in a form that can touch us and cause us
to respond, we are drawn into that true center of our
existence, and, in being drawn to that center, we are
drawn to each other. What else can happen to men
who are drawn to a single cause? Find a point of
unity—any point of unity—and you establish a unity
of spirit. Find *the* point of unity and you have found
the kingdom that is coming. This is the "body" in
which the spirit of God dwells—a plurality of persons
(note the plural form of the pronoun "you" here and
in Romans 12:1 and in 1 Cor. 3:17 and 6:19—and the
"we" of 2 Cor. 6:16) who have found their unity. It
is not the isolated individual whose "body" is the temple of God; it is the "body" that comes into being
when God's spirit rules.

And when God's spirit rules, there flows in the
veins of the newly formed "body" the vital force of
agape ("love" is such a weak translation of it) which
induces every man to share the burden of his neighbor

and transforms each individual into the hands that serve the other. Paul tries to articulate this in more detail at another point. In writing to the new congregation at Corinth (which had not yet caught the vision of this unity) he makes it clear that to him the church is a demonstration of this approaching reality. It is not an unclear symbol but a foretaste of the future, a prediction of what is to be. Paul sees the church in terms of its finest possibilities—possibilities which become real only when the spirit of God is not resisted. The little witnessing communities that Paul brought to birth in Asia Minor and Greece were symbols even at their worst, but at their best they were a glimpse of the ultimate reality that will eventually encompass us all.

That reality requires something right now of those who see it. It requires that they believe in it as the surest thing in all the world and, since believing involves behavior, it requires that they begin to live right now as though the kingdom is here.

This will not be easy. It will guarantee suffering and persecution. The last of the beatitudes will be our lot when we commit ourselves to this way. Men find their most immediate security in that which is stable and dead. When some of us begin to live as though the future holds something different, we will be resisted at every turn. We shall perhaps even die for that cause. But this suffering is the seed of tomorrow. He who will be the voice "behind us" (in Hebrew idiom, that means *the future*) saying "this is the way; walk in it" (Isa. 30:21), is the person who will precede us in the coming age.

Life is meant to be an expanding experience. Not only is the present moment to be enjoyed—it is meant to be an open doorway beckoning us to tomorrow. Let us not pause to build barns for yesterday's grain or be held up looking in the mirror to see that we please ourselves. Let us abandon ourselves to the claim that God is the *omega* as well as the *alpha*. God's world is going to its glory and our worlds are giving way to his worlds. The voice of his authority has sounded— the voice of the man who commits himself to the reality that is and shall be. Let us respond by saying, with all eagerness and anticipation, "Come! Come and declare your full Lordship!" This is the ethic that can sweep us up into a life that puts all other ethics to the service of one.

To pray *come, Lord Jesus* is to do something more than ask for the return of a dear friend who left us too soon. Yet that seems to be the sense in which a few Christians pray it. And their prayer is more a nostalgic wish than a prayer. It is nostalgic because their Jesus is only the personality who walked in the Holy Land two thousand years ago, not the Son of Man who is becoming the Lord of Lords and King of Kings by God's own will. It is no more than a wish because it does not embody the most essential element of prayer: the element of struggle.

To pray is to tangle with reality and demand from it a blessing. To be sure, one can pray to some lesser gods and even get the blessings one covets, but praying to God is wrestling with something bigger than life itself, as Jacob did. This is the meaning of the name Israel: *he is wrestling God.* The world to come is in the hands of this man, for he is the only one who really wants it.

It is characteristic for people to either fear the future or find themselves unable to even believe it. We should be people who want it badly enough to be constantly making the future into now—as God does. Why should we hesitate to embrace the future with love and fulfillment? Are we afraid that in losing the fleeting present we shall be given nothing in return? All that our spirit yearns for awaits us. It is, after all, not our selfish fantasies that await fulfillment. It is God's will that threatens to be done and God's kingdom that promises to come. It is to the future being planned by the Lord of life himself that we are invited, and he who is wise will live to constantly embrace that future in every moment of his life.

To pray *come, Lord Jesus* is to pray for fulfillment, for the realization of God's kind of love, for the realization of community. It is not to welcome just any kind of change, for some changes are merely the symptoms of our frenzy. It is to welcome the changes that God is constantly bringing on us and dare to believe that they are for our good welfare.

This is an age of frenzy. We are like a million ants about to be squashed by a mighty press bearing down on us from above. We sense the fear but do not see what it is that is about to destroy us. In our desperation we look about and see only our fellow ants. "He must be the threat," each says to himself as he spots a fellow ant, and we turn to devouring each other for fear of being devoured. When the press finally reaches us, most have already perished in mutual murder and few are left to be killed.

The enemies that press down on us are the vast mechanical gods of our own making—kingdoms so large we fail to see them, whose symbols have been so sanctified by familiarity that we believe they are the inviolable kingdom of God. Their weight and burden is felt, however, and we react with fear and panic. We turn and make wars with our fellow humans to rid ourselves of the threat, but it only increases our fears and we become a race of madmen.

If we could only let go of the kingdoms we have created! If we could only embrace the ever-evolving kingdom of God! If we could only discover the supreme value of the things that Life itself creates and, by process of discovering that, see through the shoddiness of our own created values—then move from that discovery to coveting what is supreme! If we could only bring ourselves to the point of engaging our entire being in the prayer that says *come* to God!

We would be saved.